I0214422

ARISTOTLE'S POLITICAL PHILOSOPHY

ARISTOTLE'S POLITICAL PHILOSOPHY

An Inquiry into the *Nicomachean Ethics*, *Politics*, and *Rhetoric*

MARK BLITZ

University of Notre Dame Press
Notre Dame, Indiana

Notre Dame, Indiana 46556
undpress.nd.edu

Published in the United States of America

Library of Congress Control Number: 2025948066

ISBN: 978-0-268-21098-4 (Hardback)
ISBN: 978-0-268-21101-1 (WebPDF)
ISBN: 978-0-268-21100-4 (Epub3)

GPSR Compliance Inquiries:
Lightning Source France, 1 Av. Johannes Gutenberg, 78310 Maurepas, France
compliance@lightningsource.fr | Phone: +33 1 30 49 23 42

To Ellen

CONTENTS

Part Three Speech

Introduction

The ethical and political phenomena that Aristotle examines are the starting point for all political action and understanding. My first purpose is to clarify these phenomena. My second, related purpose is to explore Aristotle's view of them, in a single work. Aristotle is the first thinker to address these phenomena directly in their own terms. He is vital in helping us disperse the contemporary haze that obscures or distorts them.

My third purpose is to examine whether today's opinions and institutions negate the importance of the phenomena Aristotle addresses or the truth of his understanding. Aristotle argues that practical happiness is achieved through ethical virtue and that virtue is linked to practical reason and to a natural, rationally comprehensible order of political excellence. But many today believe that happiness consists simply in satisfying desire. Others claim that judgment and meaning are encapsulated within various competing group identities. And some claim that morality consists of universal rules that should restrain behavior but do not constitute happiness.

Aristotle also argues that the heart of politics is a community's form of government (or "regime") and the competing claims to rule of the virtuous, wealthy, and equally free. But we today apparently are governed democratically through formal, legitimate political parties and extensive administrative bureaucracies and directed by vast "private" institutions that shape commerce, education, and public opinion. In any event, Aristotle studies the political life of slave-holding cities with perhaps at most 40,000 citizens and 150,000 inhabitants, not countries with populations in the tens or hundreds of millions. How, then, can what he examines still be significant?

In these areas and others, I show how what Aristotle examines remains the basis on which to understand and evaluate practical life.[1] Aristotle's view of ethics and politics is powerful because it uncovers what still, or necessarily, belongs to common understanding and action. The phenomena he discusses allow us to clarify what we take for granted but do not appreciate or think through and what has become occluded but is still fundamental. He makes evident what these phenomena are and how they first appear to philosophical reflection.

I discuss Aristotle's *Nicomachean Ethics*, *Politics*, and *Rhetoric*.[2] I do not offer commentaries on these works but explore the central phenomena they bring to light. I therefore sometimes use evidence from one work to clarify what is said in another, adjusting as necessary for different levels in Aristotle's arguments. Most but not all of my analyses follow the order of his presentation in the three works, and I divide my book into three parts, "Virtue," "Politics," and "Speech." I usually summarize a portion of his presentation and then follow with a discussion.

Aristotle's *Ethics*, *Politics*, and *Rhetoric* intend to improve action, but they are based on observation or contemplation. This is how Aristotle describes his activity throughout the works.[3] Indeed, he suggests that a life of observation or at least one that observes certain matters is the happiest and most divine, or pure, human life.[4] So Aristotle's intention in his practical works is not merely to improve our actions. He also means to advance theoretical activity, and he therefore often discusses matters (such as the various intellectual virtues, pleasure, and friendship) beyond what improving ordinary practice seems to require.[5]

Aristotle's Procedure

Aristotle orients his examination primarily around opinions and perplexities about these opinions, as well as other thinkers' views.

He does not begin with a demonstrative theoretical understanding, with truths from which he seeks to deduce all else. He does not claim that something is so, moreover, without showing evidence for it in ordinary understanding and in things' everyday presence and our perception of them.

This procedure is or appears reasonable because ethics, politics, and rhetoric are inseparable from what we say and believe. Ordinary perceptions and ordinary opinions are unlikely to be altogether false. They are therefore central in discovering what is true. Perplexities arise when these opinions are unclear or contradictory, but an opinion is not correct merely because nothing initially seems perplexing about it.[6] This is why Aristotle typically begins with what we say about a phenomenon, draws out perplexities in these opinions, and then turns back to the phenomenon to show directly or indirectly how these opinions are grounded in the phenomenon. This presentation, in turn, deepens, widens, and clarifies our first view of the phenomenon. Aristotle sees and describes what we ordinarily see with greater precision, complexity, or comprehensiveness than most—or almost all—of us do while remaining anchored to ordinary understanding.

Aristotle's approach is not only dialectical, however, when that means finding the higher, fuller, or truer instance of a phenomenon that resolves a contradiction by showing the partial truth of what merely resembles or belongs to it. As I said, he often proceeds this way, for example, when he considers courage, self-restraint, and friendship. But he also clarifies phenomena by discussing them in his own terms, such as activity, nature, proportion (analogy), and what is simple. When Aristotle employs such matters, however, he tries not to depart far from the phenomenon he is examining.[7]

In short, Aristotle first describes what he sees and hears as it ordinarily presents itself, but he also sometimes discusses it in the terms in which he finally describes everything. Aristotle shows what in a phenomenon—say, a virtue of character such as moderation—accounts both for our opinions and our perplexities about it. He therefore expands our understanding of the limits, range, and powers of that virtue and what makes it good.[8]

How Aristotle Teaches

Aristotle writes carefully, but his views are not simply hidden.[9] His occasional unconventional (or outrageous) suggestions are visible—consider, for example, his discussion of tyranny in the *Politics*—although they sometimes are easy to pass over. Moreover, he does not always make explicit the final steps in his discussions, intellectually or politically.[10] His discussion of philosophy, for example, does not in so many words tell us to protect it politically, although he means to show what is ordinary or useful as well as extraordinary about it. In general, Aristotle gives careful direction to the educated reader who may be defending virtue and justice and to the reader who may be philosophical or defending the philosophical life.[11] He at once elevates and calms our expectations. He raises the nobility of ethical virtue while subtly showing its dependence on others and, therefore, its limits, and he reminds his educated readers, students, potential statesmen, teachers, and fathers how arguments that clarify and extol virtues need to gain trust through specific discussions in which words match deeds. One might thus say that Aristotle means what he says but that it is not always easy to attend to and sometimes difficult to see what he is saying, especially given the dense scholarly and religious fog that surrounds his views and has only recently begun to be dissipated.

This new clarity begins at least with Hegel, advances radically with Martin Heidegger, and is developed or newly seen by several who studied with him—Hannah Arendt, Jacob Klein, and Leo Strauss, among others (and by their students and students of their students)—and by several contemporary philosophers.[12] I refer to several of their works but do not attempt to adjudicate disputes among them or emphasize differences that I have with their arguments or those of others.[13]

Part One

Virtue

Chapter One

Happiness, the Good, and the Noble

Ends

Aristotle begins his "philosophy concerning human affairs" with discussions in the *Ethics* of the good, or the human good, and happiness (*Ethics* 1094a1–2).[1] We should not take for granted the significance of this beginning: the human good is the central phenomenon. We do not understand human things by looking first toward economic affairs, loose psychological generalities, statistically significant patterns of behavior, or similar matters. And what is good does not belong to a realm of mere preference or assertion, such as a realm of "values," that is separate from what we can know. Nor do we begin by studying divine texts. "Every art and every inquiry," he claims, "and similarly every action as well as choice is opined to aim at some good" (*Ethics* 1094a2).[2] Aristotle therefore starts his inquiry where free people begin their actions: the reason why, or that for the sake of which, they act. More than this, he goes on to claim that a single end or good exists at which all human things aim and that one science exists—political science or statesmanship—that organizes the others.[3]

The claim that a single end exists at which the others aim appears difficult to uphold because the variety of things at which arts and actions aim seems daunting. Order exists in this variety, however, for arts are connected through a single power, wish, or architectonic art, as bridle makers are subservient to horsemen, cavalry subservient to generals, generals oriented to victory in war, and war oriented to the justice and preservation of the city or country.[4]

This ordering still leaves much disorganized variety, however, for if each group of arts stands on its own, our actions will finally be disordered. But if "there is some end of our actions that we wish for on account of itself," with the others wished for this end (rather than each being chosen for something else, for if this is so, then longing would finally be empty and pointless), "clearly this would be the good, that is, the best" (*Ethics* 1094a18–22). Knowledge of this overarching good would be "of great weight," so one must try to grasp what it is and to "which of the sciences or capacities it belongs" (*Ethics* 1094a25–26).

Ultimate disorder, however, seems as likely as the possibility that there must be a final, ordering end. What if disorder, however undesirable, is the truth of arts and actions? So, before he examines this end, Aristotle reminds us that a science exists that organizes the other sciences and actions, namely, statesmanship or political science (as I indicated with warfare). The legislators tell us who may do and study what. Political science is the truly architectonic art, and, indeed, the city's good is (or appears) nobler and more divine than an individual's.[5]

Discussion: Ends

Aristotle does not intend his statement that everything is oriented to some good to be visibly controversial but to indicate the proper standpoint for understanding human affairs. Indeed, despite our centuries of philosophical speculation and value relativism his suggestion is clear and commonsensical. Even idleness is meant to pass the time, deflect from serious business, or annoy. Someone who intentionally engages in random behavior does so to make a point or a splash or to validate a theory. What is good as one appeals to it rhetorically is "above all" what each chooses relative to what he is fond of, for example, victory, honor, or money.[6]

Aristotle's beginning and his subsequent examination allow us to see the basic orientation of human action that becomes constricted when we see goods merely as objects we happen to desire, as economic, or as "values." The way we now first see our choices is influenced by contemporary understanding and the way of life that embodies it. But the substance of the goods we seek cannot be occluded altogether. Aristotle will present in their fullness matters that later views narrow or from which they deflect. (This is one reason that so much of his discussion of human virtue resonates so immediately.) Aristotle begins by stating something that appears, or should appear, obvious.

We should also see, however, that Aristotle's opening is more radical than it might seem. By emphasizing that our actions aim at some good, Aristotle implicitly sets aside the view that we should first of all perform actions piously, stylishly, or with bureaucratically procedural exactitude apart from the good that may result from them. If, however, one considers such ways to themselves be chosen as goods or goals, then we (and Aristotle) have assimilated them to what is good. He has rationalized them. Justice too, which some might consider to be proper procedure, proves for Aristotle to be a virtue and, thus, among the goods that comprise the happiness that, he will argue, is the overarching good at which we aim. As Plato does in the *Republic*'s beginning conversations, Aristotle implicitly rejects the view that our good (or justice) is righteous or pious behavior apart from satisfaction. Indeed, this standpoint continues throughout the *Ethics*' first book: Aristotle examines the connection of one's happiness to the fate of one's ancestors and progeny with only the faintest suggestion of an afterlife. Separating the rational standpoint from one that starts from faith is apparently a necessary beginning for a clear look at the human good. It is easy to lose sight of this in our age, which combines the widespread irreligion of many with a tendency to leave unquestioned (and to underestimate) the religious practices and beliefs of others.

It is also true, however, that Aristotle soon argues that happiness is virtue and that virtue is noble.[7] Noble or virtuous action may not always result in what is evidently good for one: courage may cause one's death in battle, friends may renounce honors in each other's favor, and intellectual virtue downplays the ordinary goods with which ethical virtues deal. So Aristotle combines what is beautiful and good in a new way. He fits all to the good at which we aim, happiness, and he treats the pleasure that supervenes on virtue as inseparable from what makes virtue choiceworthy: pleasure belongs to any true good or aim.[8] At the same time, he assimilates what is good to a rational nobility or mode of action (i.e., ethical virtue) and to a rational divinity (philosophy).[9]

Aristotle does not make clear why all our activities are pointless if we could not orient them to one good. Could not a variety of actions be adequate if perhaps less desirable or directive than greater order? Why would not a series of partial ends—say, various bodily pleasures—relieve the problem of pointlessness? At this juncture, however, such questions suggest primarily that the substance of our end is unclear. Even seeking a variety of bodily pleasures would guide actions only because we think that they are fulfilling, or as fulfilling as possible. It is this fulfillment, or overarching good, that is our goal and the question that Aristotle has in mind in his next few chapters, and it is this question, and implicit or explicit answers to it, that is the basic standpoint for human affairs.

Precision

This imprecision about a comprehensive end may be why Aristotle reminds us in chapter 3 that we can expect knowledge but not mathematical precision from political science because what is noble and good is always disputed. (We may say that even if there is a natural good, it will not be authoritatively posited and enforced everywhere.) We can at most speak of what is largely so and neither persuade nor demonstrate mathematically. Such is true also for the suitable student of ethics and politics, who is not everyone under the sun but rather one who already governs his longings by reason. Noble and just things are held to be variable, and the simply good things for men are not always good for each of us.

Discussion: Precision

This reminder that the imprecision of human choice belongs to the subject and not to a failure of academic and bureaucratic technique is fundamental, although myriad claims to the contrary make it easy to forget. The noble and good things are inherently matters of dispute for us, and we cannot judge or effect exactly at each moment the balance between meeting necessities and advancing excellence. Attempts to obviate or ignore these disputes, or to impose rules that are supposedly valid in each case, are mistaken or dangerous.

The fact that the good and noble things are disputable, however, does not mean that choice is arbitrary. Aristotle intends to uncover reasonable guidelines for choice—happiness has substance, and some forms of government are better than others—but circumstances and the nature of what is good and just make precise, universal rules to guide actions impossible. Claims to possess exact knowledge rather than prudent understanding are likely to mask an attempt to impose one's own advantage.

Although the order of goods is imprecise, it is clear to Aristotle and to ordinary citizens that, as I said, an architectonic science exists. Political science orders which sciences are to be learned by whom and what we ought to do. Its end therefore encompasses other goals and is the human end. Still, what is this end? There is (as it turns out in chapter 4) a common name for the comprehensive good, namely, happiness, and a common home for it, the city, even if its substance is imprecise.

That happiness is such an overarching goal is especially clear if we bracket or dismiss our contemporary view that happiness is passive contentment, however achieved, and instead emphasize happiness as the complete human activity, as will Aristotle.[10]

How "overarching" political science is may be unclear, especially if we consider today's academic political scientists. A shoemaker's, physician's, and even warrior's goal is partial, however, and may conflict. If, say, war is necessary, we must risk health, commandeer commercial ships for battle or evacuation, or order shoemakers to turn their attention from elegant heels to functioning boots. It is law, and choice under it, that puts partial and sometimes conflicting ends in order and distributes means to them, and it is political science or statesmanship that is the ground for good laws and choice about who may or must do what. This is so even if we leave much choice to individuals (as we do in our American founding and in our constitutional as well as everyday laws).[11]

We should see, nonetheless, that the connection of ends and resources can be murky. Although our ends are interrelated, their order of precedence is not easily visible at every moment, especially during peace. What I must do to meet my necessities, moreover, may conflict with what is necessary politically. In fact, it is not always clear that the political goal is superior to the individual one. Is life worth risking in a foolish battle led by an inept general in an unjust war? Indeed, proper individual choice can also be ambiguous. Are many small generous acts more worthwhile than one beautiful one?[12] Although happiness is our goal and political science architectonic, happiness is complex and its relationship to political science subtle.

Aristotle resists explicitly exploring such issues. It is enough at first to remind us that various goods exist, that they fit at least roughly, that they contribute to or are arranged as happiness, and that political science (or the city and its laws) orders the goods and the arts and actions associated with them. It is enough to start roughly because, as I said, Aristotle begins and never departs very far from opinions that people actually hold and because variability in political things limits the precision of general views.

Happiness

In chapter 4 Aristotle returns from his theoretical "digression" (about precision) and names the comprehensive good. The many and the refined agree that it is happiness but disagree about its substance: for the many it is pleasure, wealth, honor, and other apparent goods.[13] Happiness does seem different for the wise, however, as Aristotle subtly indicates by digressing to examine whether we should start our investigation from the beginnings (presumably the reasons or principles that will defend opinions about happiness) or, rather, whether we should work toward them. Should we begin from what is known simply or from what is known to us?

Aristotle's choice is to begin from common sense, from what is known to "us" when we are brought up nobly. He does not describe all the elements of nobility or deduce them from some other, broader principle.

The three views of happiness are lives devoted to (bodily) pleasure, honor, and contemplation.[14] I explore these more fully later, but Aristotle indicates now that pleasure is the way of cattle, while happiness involves activity, and that honor depends on others, for we seek it from the virtuous and prudent to convince ourselves that we are good. The implication is that theoretical activity more reliably than ethical virtue is unable to be taken from one.[15] (Ethical virtue goes beyond animal perception because it involves choice and, therefore, reason directing the body and its enjoyments.)[16]

We choose happiness for its own sake: unlike health, say, we do not choose it for still other reasons. For what would these goals be that do not themselves belong to happiness? What we choose simply for its own sake is "noble." Genuine happiness is complete and lacks nothing, for whatever we lacked we would still desire.

Discussion: Happiness

Does Aristotle consider happiness's completion a single activity, or, rather, does it involve several activities that together use all our powers and enjoy all kinds of goods?[17] Is our end a perfect activity or, rather, a life that lacks nothing, including what from the noblest standpoint will include what is imperfect?[18] What is the aim if time and other resources are scarce? Aristotle is arguing that if a single activity is ultimate it would use all our powers sufficiently, for if it did not we would still lack something—unfulfilled desires, say, or truncated spiritedness or reason. The true issue is whether there is in fact such a single end or way of life, an issue that pervades his discussion. It is best now to suggest that one life, or one activity, the intellectual one as it considers the highest matters, is most noble, choiceworthy, and complete but that it is not for everyone, for most lack the leisure and resources necessary for it.

Aristotle discusses the link between happiness and intellectual virtue in the *Ethics*' final book and describes there the elements of happiness more fully. Happiness is an activity choiceworthy for its own sake: it is the end of human concern. And it is self-sufficient. Complete happiness, moreover, is the activity of what naturally rules and possesses intelligence about the whole and is the virtue belonging to the best. This is contemplation and intellectual virtue: it is intelligence about the noble and divine; it is the divine, or most divine, in us; it is the most continuous; it is the greatest pleasure; and it is the most self-sufficient—the least in need of necessities or of others, even if it is better together with others.

Ethical virtue, the next highest way of life, is less singular. It proves to be multiple in itself, for the peaks of practical life—greatness of soul, justice, and friendship—are not identical. Yet even theoretical activity is restricted by necessities. And although someone with contemplative excellence meets his necessities virtuously, it is unclear if he is sufficiently just (or friendly or magnanimous) if he does not also turn to political and ethical advising or founding. One activity is happiest—both noble or choiceworthy in itself and least incomplete—but only in the best circumstances for one with the fullest individual powers.[19]

Both ethical and intellectual virtue are outstanding and pleasurable and if they exist in their fullness, rare. Being rare (or striking or outstanding) and pleasant are, together with being fitting, elements of what is noble or beautiful. True happiness is noble and complete: we choose it for its own sake; it is outstanding; it is fitting, because everything in virtue is measured or "true"; it is pleasant, because all virtuous activity is pleasant; and it is complete in its active use of our powers.[20] Aristotle does not specify all these elements of the noble. He concentrates instead on its being for its own sake and its being the completeness of our human work. The elements of pleasure, fit, and being rare or outstanding, however, become central in his understanding of the virtues. Ethical virtue is noble because it is prominent or rare (as greatness of soul), pleasurable, and measured.[21]

Let us consider further Aristotle's statement about the three ways of life. Happiness as bodily pleasure does not differentiate us from other animals. We too nourish ourselves and perceive, but we also think. Ethical virtue goes beyond animal perception because it involves choice and, therefore, reason directing the body and its enjoyments.[22] Aristotle's dismissing the view that happiness consists of bodily pleasure, however, does not mean that he ignores pleasure. On the contrary: one virtue, moderation, concerns the measured choice of bodily pleasures, and both ethical and intellectual virtue are pleasant in their own way. Acting ethically is pleasant, and what is simply good is simply pleasant for those for whom what is good simply is good for them.[23]

Aristotle's dismissing the opinion that happiness is devotion to bodily pleasure while acknowledging that each virtue (and not only moderation) is connected to pleasure distinguishes him from the modern view that happiness is the satisfaction of desire, the relief from unease, or the movement of desire from one object to another. This view suggests that pleasures are all commensurable. In Aristotle's understanding, however, pleasures are differentiated by the activity that brings them, and what is good is not what satisfies undifferentiated desire or longing. To achieve the fullest happiness one cannot simply add pleasures, whatever their source.

Were all pleasures commensurable, the pleasure from seeing three or six or ten flowers could equal the pleasure from hearing Delibes's *Flower Duet*, or the pleasure from a jug of wine drunk quickly all by oneself could outweigh the pleasure from several generous acts. Such equating is based on views about desire and satisfaction that overturn or largely modify Aristotle's view. We can best recognize and evaluate this change by beginning from his direct, visible understanding. The substance of pleasure itself and why pleasure seems sometimes to lead to unrestraint are important questions for Aristotle. But his starting point and, commonsensically, ours is to see the connection of different pleasures to different activities.

A life governed by ethical virtue is, as I mentioned, the second understanding of happiness. At first, it seems to be devoted to honor or distinction, but honor (or reputation) can be given by the wrong people for the wrong reasons. In fact, one wishes or should wish to be honored for virtuous character and virtuous actions. More directly, honor points to happiness as the political life, which Aristotle treats as requiring a virtuous character, one comprised of each of the virtues. He therefore treats greatness of soul, or great pride—the proper seeking and holding of honor—as the comprehensive peak of moral virtue, the beautiful ornament of the others.[24] He also shows how justice (and, therefore, the disposition to be just) is comprehensive and how the peak of friendship involves full virtue. I will discuss these ambiguities in due course, but we should recognize that statesmanship constitutes happiness and that Aristotle understands the right kind of political life to be one governed by and for ethical virtue. He also makes this clear in the *Politics* and the *Rhetoric.* "The virtue of man and citizen is necessarily the same in the best city" (*Politics* 1288a39). Hence—with the unusual exception of theoretical excellence—happiness is ethical, or political, virtue.

This is remarkable and perplexing from the modern standpoint, but from another point of view, obvious. Neither Christian virtues nor Kantian moralism suggest that the statesman's life is one of moral excellence or even a human peak. Kant takes pains to show how political lying can and should be overcome; that is, he takes pains to show how politics may be moral but not that it more fully than other activities allows or exemplifies moral choice.[25] Indeed, the virtues are not for him morality's heart. Christian virtues and faith, moreover, are not exemplified by, or, indeed, may conflict with, great pride and other virtues. In contrast, a look at Churchill, Lincoln, or Washington makes visible why, counter to these views, statesmanship is a human peak or "happiness."

We may also suggest that acting ethically (for a long enough period) is happiness or is complete because it deals with all of the ordinary goods that we seek to enjoy. Its overarching practical aim (a virtuous character) encompasses lesser aims. As I said, happiness is not ease or contentment but, rather, activity, and activity involves dealing in a measured or fitting way with pleasure, wealth, beauty, honor, speech, friends, and the passions connected to these goods.[26] Aristotle's is not a morality that eschews but a character that considers, chooses, uses, and enjoys. His understanding of virtue is not oriented around the notions of self-denying restraint or mere permission to act that make the notion that moral virtue is happiness seem strange. Moral virtue is not the enemy of pleasure; on the contrary, we cannot reasonably understand happiness to eschew pleasure. Happiness as the proper way to enjoy goods, that is, virtue, perforce enjoys these goods.[27]

We may supplement Aristotle's view of happiness here (and of people's view of it) with his discussion in the *Rhetoric*. Rhetoric exhorts and dissuades, and one of its elements is to convince those who deliberate in the assembly to take particular courses of action. It therefore involves what people believe, and their view of what is conducive or contrary to happiness is especially important. Happiness, Aristotle suggests in the *Rhetoric*, is pretty much agreed on by all to be one or more of these: faring well with virtue, self-sufficiency, pleasure with security, and abundant possessions with the ability to act with and guard them. Happiness thus involves various goods: external ones such as friends and wealth, goods of the body such as health, and internal goods such as virtues of soul. In the *Rhetoric*, Aristotle lists prudence, courage, moderation, and justice.[28] What is missing are elements of the more complete list of ethical and intellectual virtues he soon elaborates in the *Ethics*. As I suggested, his understanding expands but does not simply depart from the ordinary view.[29]

The Good

Let us return to the *Ethics*. Aristotle mentions but does not discuss the theoretical life in detail in Book I. But he displays it, and its utility, in the next chapter, where he criticizes others' understanding of what is good. His point is to separate the human good—the human end—from a possible good as such.

In particular, in the sixth chapter of Book I, Aristotle questions whether a universal good or an idea of good exists, as argued by those who introduced the forms: Plato and his student Eudoxus. While doing this, Aristotle continues to discuss the goods at which things aim, brings out the complexity of trying to begin from first principles (the whys or reasons) rather than from what is first for us, and subtly indicates the oddness of theoretical activity and how to deal with it politically. Aristotle justifies his criticism of Plato by suggesting that it is more pious for philosophers to honor truth first, rather than friendship, or their own. This proper divinity characterizes the theoretical life and separates it from other lives where, presumably, friendship and one's own are paramount.[30]

Aristotle raises perplexities by questioning the ideas' proponents. He claims that there are as many ways of saying "good" as of saying "is": what something is, for example, a man or a god;[31] what sort it is (its quality), for example, virtuous; how much it is (its quantity), for example, measured; its relations, for example, useful; and its time and place, for example, the right time and place. What, then, could the common or universal good be? Moreover, no single science of (even) these goods exists: the right time, say, differs for physicians and generals. Moreover, if there is a good itself, it would need to cover equally any good thing, but what is eternally white is no whiter than the ephemeral. The good, then, would not only be the eternal.

Some proponents of the forms might reply that there is a single form only for goods that we cherish for themselves, say, prudence, seeing, and honor, but not for all that produce them. If only the idea (of the good) is good in itself, however, then these others seem pointless. If not, each of these is equally good, and there is no common idea. Nor do these goods all stem from or contribute to one good. Rather, they are perhaps all called good by analogy, as sight for the body is analogous to prudence for the soul. In any event, Aristotle concludes, pursuing this issue belongs to a "different philosophy" (i.e., different from contemplating the political), and such a good would not be relevant for action or possession.

Discussion: The Good

Aristotle's discussion leaves open the relations among the perfections of different things, that is, how independent they and their ends are.

Aristotle's chief present argument with Plato, it seems to me, is with this question of substance and substantive order: "good," primarily, is everywhere analogous or alike as something's full or complete (and choiceworthy) working and activity, what arises from this (e.g., pleasure), what stems from it, and the means to it. The substance of this varies among things (a cow's vs. a horse's vs. a house's vs. a shoe's look, material, food, etc.). It is clear enough, say, that the right time for the general's attack is not simply independent, but is also subservient to the statesman's purpose. But in what way and to what degree are independent perfections ordered? Both plants and animals in one sense have an independent perfection, but as Aristotle says in the *Politics*' first book, plants are for the sake of animals and they for our sake—for our food and clothes—"if nature makes nothing that is incomplete or purposeless."

Aristotle does not confront here the Platonic thought that some members of a class, the various beautiful things, say, seek to be and in this way imitate or reflect the idea, say, beauty, simply. Goods that are not simply good for us, as Aristotle sees this, are not inferior imitations in the Platonic sense but, rather (when they are not merely means to other ends), are "good" by being analogous to what is simply good. Inferior, that is, insufficient, pleasures and activities are good by analogy. (This inferiority is one reason that a "good" thief, say, is not truly good.) Philosophy is seemingly not erotic, as Plato sometimes presents it. Moreover, as Aristotle indicates, he does not develop precisely what analogy is or what makes it possible. We may note that analogy is a version of likeness, of being alike, which is one way to understand Plato's view of the relation between an idea and its members.

Aristotle's emphasis on what is good is a fundamental reminder of the central source of meaning and direction for our activities. They have or seek an end, whatever the importance of mere obedience and whatever the prevalence of passivity and thoughtlessness. The human good is the lodestar of action, however much sophistication occludes this basic fact. The question, then, is the substance of this good—happiness—and Aristotle now begins to consider more fully the elements that belong to it.

Elements of Happiness

Having indicated the usual opinions about happiness and having criticized theoretical views of what is good, Aristotle (in chapter 7) returns to the architectonic good he is seeking. This good would be the complete end related to all actions as, say, victory is to war. If there is one or several complete ends, these would be best. The complete is what we seek for itself; the "simply" complete is always so sought and never on account of something else.[32] We always choose happiness for itself and never on account of something else. We choose pleasure, intellect, honor, and every virtue for themselves, and as bringing happiness. Moreover, the complete good is held to be self-sufficient; that is, it makes life choiceworthy and needs nothing extra. "Sufficient" means sufficient for oneself, one's family, and one's fellow citizens, for "by nature a human being is political" (*Ethics* 1097b11). As Aristotle suggests in the *Politics*, moreover, "it is impossible for a city to be happy" unless "most people or all of its parts are happy" (*Politics* 1264b18–22). Evenness can exist in the whole but in neither part, but this is not so for happiness.[33] Happiness is complete, self-sufficient, and actions' end.

Aristotle has still more to say about happiness generally. A thing's good resides in its work. Is there a work of a human being as there is of a shoemaker, or our eyes? Living, nutrition, and growth are common to plants and animals, and sense perception is common to animals. What remains (as human) is the practice of what has reason, that is, what thinks and obeys thought: "the work of a human being is an activity of soul in accord with reason" (*Ethics* 1098a14). The serious man acts nobly, with virtue, and brings matters to completion.[34] The human good, therefore, is an activity of soul with virtue, or the best and most complete one, according with or obeying reason, and it is virtue for a complete life or time: the superiority in virtue completes the human work.

Discussion: Elements of Happiness

We should see that by an "end," Aristotle means more than a goal, aim, or purpose external to an activity. An end can indeed be a goal or an aim but only because it completes or perfects. As such, the end pervades and is integrated into the activity. An end, here, is also not a final touch on a largely finished production, a mere stopping point (such as resting and going on to something else), or being over with (such as a rainstorm that ends.) An end, here, is what completes or fulfills. In this sense it is the beginning that gathers the related actions that participate in or serve it and gives them their direction or meaning. An end, as what allows something's burgeoning, is the starting point that directs what fulfills it. Happiness or virtue is a principle or beginning as what we are for the sake of, that is, our end.[35] Being at work in something's end is what Aristotle means by its activity, and completely being at work in its activity is its virtue. Something's end, together with its form or look, its order, is what primarily separates or limits it with regard to other things.

Aristotle's discussion of happiness as an end helps clarify our loose talk of ends, purposes, "values," and goals. Such talk makes evident the importance of these phenomena for understanding our activity and direction. But vagueness about or misinterpretation of these phenomena skews this direction and obfuscates our genuine goals.

Goods

The truth about our human good (happiness) should harmonize with what we say about it, Aristotle begins the *Ethics*' eighth chapter. As we saw in the *Rhetoric*, there are external goods and goods of body and soul; both opinion and philosophy say that goods involving the soul's activities "are the most authoritative." Happiness is viewed as virtue, prudence, a certain wisdom, and pleasure. For lovers of virtue and justice, just and virtuous things are pleasant, as horses and plays are to horse and theater lovers. For the many, pleasant things do battle, but for "the lovers of what is noble, the things pleasant by nature are pleasant." (We see here another reason that for Aristotle happiness cannot be an aimless accretion of a variety of pleasures.) Indeed, "no one would say" that someone who does not delight in just or liberal actions is just or liberal. Especially for someone serious, nobly judging actions in accord with virtue is pleasant, good, and noble. "Happiness . . . is the best, noblest, and most pleasant thing"—the best activities or the best one among them (*Ethics* 1099a25). To be happy, however, one also requires "external goods"; it is difficult or impossible to act nobly without equipment, that is, instruments such as "friends, wealth, and political power." And one cannot call happy those, say, who are "altogether ugly," or solitary (*Ethics* 1099b1–2). Moreover, one also needs a complete life without disastrous fortune or a wretched end.[36] Although happiness is divine, furthermore, it does not arise through divine fate but through "virtue and a certain learning or practice" (*Ethics* 1099b15–16). "It is reasonable" that we acquire happiness this way if "what accords with nature is naturally noblest," and if it accords with the best art or cause rather than chance (*Ethics* 1099b22–23).

Aristotle supplements his discussion of goods here with a list in his *Rhetoric*. Many speeches concern what is advantageous or harmful to the community. The list therefore includes the goods that are "pretty much" agreed on (although courage is disputed)—for example, what the prudent are inclined to prefer and "above all" what each chooses relative to what he is fond of, for example, victory, honor, or money. The point here and in the *Ethics* is that Aristotle does not merely discuss ends, or dispute theories about what is good, but also outlines goods that, as means to or elements of our goals, remain visible and visibly sought after. Attempts to dismiss such goods (say, victory or having sufficient resources, to be replaced by pacifism and poverty) work against and therefore must argue against their still compelling—because fundamental to human activity—attraction. His argument is connected as well to the commonsensical view that a complete life without awful fortune or a disastrous finish is significant for happiness. Good fortune does not guarantee or bestow happiness, however, because our natural end requires learning, habituation, and activity, as Aristotle clarifies in succeeding chapters.

One might wonder how to choose among goods that apparently conflict. Aristotle discusses this in Book I, chapter 7, of the *Rhetoric*. One chooses the greater good. What is greater, however, when two things are both advantageous? What is central is to choose what is choiceworthy for its own sake, that is, an end. One element that guides choice, thus, is self-sufficiency: this does not need that. The product and longings of the noble, better, and more choiceworthy, moreover, are nobler, better, or more choiceworthy, as are sciences with noble subjects, what we affirm prudently to be better, for example, courage rather than strength, suffering rather than doing injustice, the more rather than the less pleasant, and the stable and long-lasting. “The nobler is either what is pleasant or choiceworthy in itself” (*Rhetoric* 1369b10). Greater too are the rare, what comes from one’s own nature, what is useful for someone and for many things, the pleasant and free of pain, what makes the whole greater, and to be versus to seem, for example, being versus seeming to be wealthy.[37]

In addition to this, Aristotle discusses elements of what is greater more generally: if this, say, health, is contained in that, say, life, but not vice versa, that is greater. And what is greater can be “a proportion: between the superiority of one class to another and the greatest things within them.” These are the greater goods as rhetoric exhorts and dissuades (i.e., perhaps only some truly are greater).

Pleasure

A serious discussion of happiness must consider that our good is pleasure and not merely dismiss it as likening us to other animals. Indeed, Aristotle claims that ethical and intellectual virtue are pleasurable—for if not, how could they constitute happiness? More than this, for lovers of virtue, the things pleasant by nature are pleasant. The virtues and their pleasures do not conflict; a virtuous character and virtuous actions are noble even if some virtues (greatness of soul and justice) are superior to others in scope. Virtue’s pleasures, however, differ from the pleasures of satisfying bodily desire, and while virtuous pleasures supervene on virtuous activities, virtue’s pleasures are neither the goal nor a part of virtue itself.

What, then, is pleasure? Aristotle discusses it at length in Books VII and X of the *Ethics* and in the *Rhetoric*. The discussions have somewhat different purposes, but in my view the overall argument is the same.[38] We begin with his statement in the *Rhetoric*: "Let our premise be that pleasure is a certain motion of the soul and a concentrated perceptible settling into the soul's underlying natural condition, where pain is the opposite" (*Rhetoric* 1369b33–35). "Entering into the natural state is for the most part pleasant" (*Rhetoric* 1370a14). Force and necessity are therefore painful, as are intense efforts and serious concerns, unless "habit makes them pleasant." Play and freedom from toil are pleasant. And there is pleasure in imaginations, memories, and hopes, which are weak perceptions of some experience; pleasure is in the present perception.

Aristotle then discusses specific pleasures. "The starting point of love for everyone" takes pleasure in the presence of the beloved and also takes pleasure in remembering him and feels pain in the beloved's absence. And there is pleasure in vengeance and victory—"for where there is rivalry there is victory"—and in honor, reputation, friendships, flattery, frequent actions, and change. Moreover, pleasure exists in learning and wondering, "for in wonder there is a desire to learn such that the object of wonder is an object of desire, and in learning there is a coming into one's natural state" (*Rhetoric* 1371a31–35). And pleasure exists in benefiting and being benefited and in imitation (painting and poetry): because "both learning and wondering are pleasant," one is pleased by the inference that this is that, even if the imitated is unpleasant. And there is pleasure in events that evoke wonder, for example, being suddenly saved. So "what accords with nature is pleasant," as is what is akin (e.g., human to human) and, hence, also self-love. So too one's own things—deeds, speeches, children—are pleasant. And because "ruling is very pleasant, it is pleasant also to be held to be wise, for being prudent is the mark of a ruler and wisdom is knowledge of many wondrous things (*Rhetoric* 1371b27–29).[39]

In *Ethics* VII, chapters 11 through 14, Aristotle discusses pleasure, because "contemplating what concerns pleasure and pain belongs to him who philosophizes about statesmanship. For he is the architect of the end with a view to which we speak of each thing as being bad or good simply" (*Ethics* 1152b1–4). We sometimes hold pleasure to be not seriously worthwhile, but this does not mean that pleasure is not good: goods are either good simply or for a person, as are natures, habits, and motions. One part of our good is an activity, another a habit: restorative pleasures (e.g., quenching thirst) are pleasant only incidentally, but the activity of our unimpaired nature and habits is "unaccompanied by pain and desire." "As the various pleasant things stand in relation to one another, so do the pleasures arising from them" (*Ethics* 1153b6–9). Indeed, everyone, reasonably, weaves pleasure into happiness. All animals and humans pursue pleasure but, seemingly, different pleasures. Yet this is perhaps not the pleasure they presume but the same one. "For all things by nature possess something of the divine" (*Ethics* 1153b32–33).[40]

We trust truth more when we can explain why something false appears true. Bodily pleasures appear more choiceworthy than others because they expel pain, can cure deficient natures, are intense, and are pursued by those who cannot enjoy other pleasures. "But the pleasures unaccompanied by pain do not have an excess, and these fall among the things pleasant by nature and not incidentally" (*Ethics* 1154b15–17). Things pleasant by nature "prompt . . . action belonging to a healthy nature" (*Ethics* 1154b20). If someone's nature is simple, the same actions would always be pleasant, as "the god always enjoys a pleasure that is one and simple" (*Ethics* 1154b26). Our nature, however, is complex. There is an activity both of motion and of motionlessness, "and pleasure resides more in rest than in motion." Change is or seems sweet because of a defect: "the nature in need of change is defective" and is "neither simple nor decent."

Book X of the *Ethics* discusses pleasure especially in relation to intellectual virtue.[41] Some say pleasure is good; others, bad. In this regard, deeds carry more conviction than arguments. When they are too discordant they undermine truth. True arguments and precise distinctions are useful, for when they harmonize with deeds they prompt those who understand them to live in accord with them. Aristotle's arguments in chapters 2 and 3 of Book X and his discussion of Eudoxus there point to pleasure being a good but not the only one. In Eudoxus's correct view, all seek pleasure, avoid pain, and choose it for itself: its addition makes anything better. But this is true when any good is accompanied by another, as pleasure is by prudence.[42]

Pleasure is defined, yet admits of degrees, as do health and other goods. Moreover, feeling it is neither quick nor slow, as opposed to entering the activity that yields it: it is not a motion. Some pleasures replenish the body, but many pleasures (e.g., learning, smell, memory) are free of pain and do not replenish. And pleasure from what is noble differs in form from the shameful. An unjust man cannot feel pleasure from just actions, as an unmusical man cannot from music; shameful pleasures do not show that pleasure is not good. Moreover, many things exist that we take seriously even without pleasure, for example, seeing and knowing. So after going through largely unnamed or unreferenced opinions, Aristotle concludes that pleasure is not the good, nor is every pleasure choiceworthy, but that some are and differ from others in form.

In chapter 4 Aristotle takes up pleasure "from the beginning." This proves to be a discussion in terms of motion, completeness, and activity. Pleasure, like seeing, is complete or whole in form. Hence, it is not a motion, unlike, say, building, which moves to accomplish its end. Something complete lacks nothing with a view to its task. "It is not possible to find a motion that is complete in its form at any given moment but, if ever, only in the whole time involved" (*Ethics* 1174a27–29). The forms of motion are from which and to which. As opposed to such motion, pleasure is whole and complete, and, as with numerical units, there is no coming into being.

Sense perception is active in relation to what it perceives and, as is true of all activity, is completely active when in good condition relative to the noblest things in its purview. With such perception there is a corresponding pleasure; this is also so of thinking and contemplation. Pleasure completes not as inherent, however, but as supervening (as an add-on), like youth's bloom. That is, pleasure is not an element of the activity itself, although it is inseparable from it. Activities dim and are not continuous: so too with pleasure. Each finds choiceworthy the activity at which he especially aims—music, thought, and so on—and the pleasure connected with this. The active life and pleasure differ but are yoked together and cannot be separated.

Chapter 5 of Book X continues Aristotle's discussion of pleasures and various activities, their links and differences. We see again the power of his simple descriptions and his attempt to depict matters in terms that do not reduce everything to what is superior (say, philosophy or ethical virtue) while still recognizing the difference between high and low, or rare and ordinary. Different activities and natural and made things are completed by things different in form, so the pleasures that complete them also differ. They are bound up with and help increase the activity; to engage in, say, geometry pleasantly is to be better, longer lasting, and more precise in it. And we also see that pleasures from activities can impede each other—speech versus the aulos's pleasure, for example—as do pains. What appears good and pleasurable to someone mature is good: virtue and the good human being are the measure of each thing. The pleasures that complete the activities of the complete and blessed man are the authoritative ones that belong to a human being.

Discussion: Pleasure

Aristotle's complex understanding of pleasure, as is true of Plato's, especially in the *Philebus*, uncovers the central elements of the phenomenon. He describes the experience of pleasure itself and the connection of different pleasures to different activities. He does not attempt to reduce pleasure to material components, to make all pleasures more or less of an identical material, or to equate the worth of all pleasure as pleasure. This clarifies, or should clarify, the ground for subsequent views and for disputes with Aristotle's analysis. Aristotle's remarks in the *Ethics* and the *Rhetoric* show us both the deep and the ordinary view of pleasure. Ordinary views may not be precise, but an argument that separates a phenomenon too far from what is ordinary is untrustworthy. Some pleasures come into being as replenishments that restore a natural state: these are the pleasures that satisfy bodily needs. The pleasures that most concern Aristotle, however, are concomitant with activities such as virtue or, even, more ordinary pursuits such as seeing and hearing. Pleasure, not pain, is good but not pleasures that arise from what is depraved. As I have said before, the connection of pleasure to specific activities means that one cannot add them as if each pleasure is identical and differs only by degree.

Aristotle does not describe the elements of full (i.e., nonrestorative) pleasure in any detail. It is a perception of a concentrated settling and, as other perceptions, occurs all at once, in the moment or, even, in intellectual pleasure, perhaps outside of or not measurable by time. It may be intense. This perception belongs together with the completion of activities but differs from the activity itself, as the pleasure in knowing differs from knowing. Pleasure adds to, or supervenes on, activity.[43]

Chapter Two

The Virtues

Their Characteristics and Substance

The General Features of Virtue, I

In Book I, chapter 13, of the *Ethics*, Aristotle begins his turn to ethical virtue per se by offering a truncated discussion of the soul that also subtly indicates areas with which intellectual but not political virtue deal. The true statesman "seems to have labored" over what virtue is, "for he wishes to make citizens good and obedient to the laws," and the human good—happiness, human virtue—is an "activity of soul." So the statesman must contemplate the soul and know it with the precision sufficient for what he seeks.

The soul has one nonrational part and one with reason. A vegetative power exists in the nonrational part that causes nutrition and growth, and there is virtue but not a human virtue in this. But "there is a certain other nature in the soul" that obeys reason, say, in someone self-restrained, and "perhaps" heeds reason's commands even "more readily" in those who are moderate and courageous "since then it is in all respects in harmony with reason."[1] This part of the nonrational soul that can heed reason is characterized by desire and longing.[2] In this way it shares "somehow" in reason (as one does when heeding fathers and friends) but not as mathematics does. It is "persuaded" by reason—by criticism and exhortation.[3] If we must, we could also say that reason is twofold: what has it authoritatively and what can listen to it. So, too, is virtue distinguished: wisdom, comprehension, and prudence are intellectual; and liberality and moderation, ethical. Ethical virtues comprise character; both ethical and intellectual virtues are praiseworthy.[4]

Discussion: The General Features of Virtue, I

Aristotle's discussion reminds us how central character is for happiness. The ethical virtues as a group comprise character, and it is plausible to consider good character the basis for happiness because it deals properly with the goods we seek to enjoy. Later discussions that emphasize satisfying desire or that consider morality primarily a check on desire downplay and yet implicitly take for granted this basic phenomenon at the root of human happiness and action. Ethical virtue may help others, but it is primarily for one's own nobility: it is not or not only "morality" as we now think of it. Good character is still visible, indeed central, as a goal in rearing children, and although our view of character can shade into the moral simply, we still recognize it as fundamental in comprising happiness.

Aristotle's discussion of the soul is limited here to what he requires to show the place of reason in all virtue and to distinguish reason's activity in ethical virtue from its activity in intellectual virtue. It is not a complete discussion of reason or the soul. In general, Aristotle limits his analysis of general or higher matters to what he needs to clarify the phenomenon being discussed. For his examination here is "not so we may know what virtue is, but so that we may become good" (*Ethics* 1103b27–28). He also makes clear the place of persuasion, or reasonable persuasion, in guiding us to virtuous habits and actions.[5]

The General Features of Virtue, II

In Book II Aristotle turns to ethical virtue generally before discussing specific virtues. Intellectual virtue arises through teaching;

ethical virtue, through habit.[6] Virtues are present to those with a nature to receive them and are completed through habituation. We become virtuous by engaging in activities, unlike, say, sense perception whose powers we have and then activate. That is, we become just, moderate, and courageous by doing just, moderate, and courageous things: legislators wish to make citizens good by habituating them, and in good regimes they do this well.[7] (We therefore see the importance for virtue of just political regimes. Indeed, virtue is the goal of the best regimes.) How we conduct ourselves in fearsome circumstances makes us courageous or cowardly, as house builders become good by building well. Habits result from the activities akin to them, so the whole difference is how one is habituated from childhood.[8]

Given this, what in outline—in outline because actions are not stationary and particulars do not fall under art or precepts but pertain to the opportune moment—can one say about virtuous action? Generally, it is "acting in accord with correct reason." What does this mean? Aristotle claims that one should use manifest things as witnesses on behalf of the immanifest. Excess and deficiency naturally destroy strength and health, while proportionate amounts "create, increase and preserve health." This is also true of the virtues: "Moderation and courage are indeed destroyed by excess and deficiency, but they are preserved by the mean" (*Ethics* 1104a25–27). As I suggested, the mean or the measured belongs to the noble because it constitutes or is central to what is fitting.

Aristotle turns next to some of virtue's other elements. With virtue one enjoys or is not pained by what one ought. With virtuous deeds, moreover, unlike the arts, both the deed and the doer must be in the proper state. (That is, there must be steady choice or intention in acting virtuously.)[9] The just or moderate man comes into being by doing just and moderate things, many times: one does not become good through argument, supposing one is "philosophizing." Listening to physicians and doing nothing prescribed does not bring about a good body: "so too [one] will not have a soul in good condition by philosophizing in this way" (*Ethics* 1105b16–18).[10]

Virtue is not a passion such as desire, anger, fear, confidence, envy, joy, love, hatred, yearning, emulation, or pity. Nor is it a power we possess naturally by which we can undergo these passions. Rather, it is a habit through which we are in a good or bad state in reference to the passions—for example, feeling anger in a measured, not (excessively) intense or weak, way. We are not praised about passions themselves but in reference to virtues, which also involve choice, as passions do not, and habits, not movement (as passions do). Virtue, moreover, causes its work to be done well, as an eye's virtue makes it and its work excellent. If this is so in all cases, then a human being's virtue would be that "habit from which a human being becomes good" and from which his own work is well demonstrated.

One may also "contemplate" virtue's nature, so Aristotle expands his remarks on the mean. In everything continuous and divisible we can grasp the more, less, and equal in reference to the thing, or to us. The equal is a middle between excess and deficiency, between the numerical extremes, or a middle in relation to us. The mean preserves the good state, and good craftsmen look to this; there is nothing to take from or add to works in a good state. Virtue and nature, indeed, are more precise than any art.[11] In ethical virtue we should feel pleasure and pain "when one ought, and at the things one ought, in relation to those people with whom one ought, for the sake of what and as one ought: all these constitute the middle and what is best" and "similarly in the case of actions" (*Ethics* 1106b21–22). "Virtue," therefore, "is a habit with choice, in the mean relative to us, a habit defined by reason and as the prudent person would define it" (*Ethics* 1106b36–1107a2).

Does this general statement about the mean harmonize with the particulars? Here Aristotle proceeds by briefly discussing individual virtues. Courage is a mean concerning fear and confidence: excessive fearlessness is nameless; excessive confidence is recklessness; excessively being afraid and deficiently feeling confidence is cowardice. With bodily pleasure the mean is moderation, the excess licentiousness, the deficiency nameless—Aristotle names it insensitivity. He then continues with liberality, magnificence, greatness of soul, ambition (loving honor), anger, truthfulness, wit, and friendliness. Aristotle's point here is to show that virtue is a mean and to indicate what is hitherto nameless. It is a task to be serious, to, in each case, grasp the middle concerning the whom, how much, when, for the sake of, what, and how. "What is done well is rare, praiseworthy, and noble" (*Ethics* 1109a29–30). It is hard to be precise, but one can at least grasp the least of the bad things and drag oneself to the middle, away from one's natural inclination.[12]

Discussion: The General Features of Virtue, II

To argue that virtue is a habit is to say that it is not equivalent to or rooted in a feeling such as pity or compassion. To say that it requires correct reason (prudence) is to say that it is not equivalent to following or obeying a (divine) command or law. To say that it is not a naturally inborn power that activates itself is to say that it is not an inborn sense or conscience. To say that it is not an art is to say that virtuous action does not as such make, produce, or repair something outside itself. Aristotle's argument thus differs from subsequent views of moral action that ground it in a moral sense such as compassion, in a divine voice, or in a moral law of the sort that Kant discusses. Rather, virtues, virtuous habits, must be taught. They mold or direct what is natural: they are not concocted. Virtuous actions are the proper enjoyment of the passions we have and the goods we seek. As such, they are reasonable, directed by prudence, by practical wisdom. The goods and powers that virtues direct are not invented but are those that we recognize today even if our recognition is occluded because we look through a religious or intellectually generated way of life. Together, the virtues comprise character, or good character.[13] Moreover, discussions that trace moral actions to, say, pity or conscience must first have in mind these actions themselves, how we should describe them, and their immediate origins and links. We can forget or ignore these origins, but this stunts the understanding that governs later accounts. What morality demands of us is first seen in the phenomena that Aristotle discusses. Virtue is not "morality" when morality means limiting or controlling enjoying and seeking goods by observing general rules such as never to lie, steal, or break faith.[14]

Aristotle's list of virtues is not arbitrary but follows from our passions and the wealth, honor, and friendship that we seek or employ. Why does dealing with these virtuously constitute happiness, however, and why is virtuous action measured action, or action in the mean? Aristotle's examples indicate other places where what is measured is choiceworthy. The measured leaves neither excess nor deficiency. Excess or deficiency with regard to what, however—to use, say, or, rather, to beauty? In a product such as a chair or house good use is clear, but beauty, and the priority between beauty and use, is not. Virtue concerns one's own beauty (nobility) of character, and what is measured or fitting is an element of the noble. Virtue also ennobles, or usefully serves, the common good, although its nobility and utility may not be identical, especially for intellectual virtue.[15] We cannot measure virtuous actions precisely. But they are no more arbitrary than are fitting words, persuasive speeches, or just and advantageous political actions. They belong to a whole—here the choice of a noble or humanly excellent disposition or set of dispositions. And, as measured, virtuous actions are seen and judged by reason. We may also say that excess (or deficiency) in any area restricts virtuous action in other areas and, therefore, restricts the proper dealing with human goods simply and overall. As I have said, the virtues as a whole comprise character as a whole.

The virtuous action is not measured in relation to an absolute or general law. This absence does not make it arbitrary, however, because choice in terms of virtuous habits is not arbitrary. But prudent choice of virtuous action does mean that circumstances make virtuous actions (but not virtue itself) variable and that full virtue requires equipment—wealth, say, or political office—that is not equally available to all. Unlike morality grounded in moral law, pity, or conscience, virtue in the fullest sense is not universally available. Still, courage, moderation, liberality, and other virtues are accessible, and even limited magnificence and magnanimity are obtainable within one's circumstances.

Aristotle's brief statement that legislators wish to make citizens good indicates the importance for virtue of just political regimes. This issue becomes thematic in the *Politics* and is addressed in various places in the *Ethics*. I discuss this below. Here we should see that this natural link remains powerful but is obscured today in at least four ways in our liberal democratic regime: the general understanding of forming character and of religion as private more than public, happiness seen as satisfying private desire, the wish to restrict government's interference in private affairs, and concern with partisan excess and inferior government. Yet, as I will suggest, liberal democracy too is pointed toward and requires a certain character that we advance in education, in criminal and other law, and in forming families and what they teach. This link is fundamental even if it is prudent to limit the activities of often harmful governments.

The Voluntary

Book III begins with five chapters on what is voluntary.[16] It clarifies the central issues from the standpoint of judgment and use, not from a theory that aligns directly with contemporary discussions.[17] What is forced on us (and, therefore, involuntary) are not the things for the sake of which we act but, rather, those whose origin is not in us but external. Acting in ignorance of principles, where this ignorance causes one's corruption (say, one's injustice), is blameworthy and differs from involuntary ignorance of particulars.

In the second chapter Aristotle turns to choice, which "distinguishes characters more than actions." Choice is central to virtue. Choice is not shared by nonrational animals, does not stem from desire or spiritedness, and differs from wish, which may be for what one cannot bring about or for ends, while choice is for what is related to ends.[18] Nor is choice opinion, which concerns all things and what is false and true. Chapter 3 concerns deliberation. We deliberate about what is up to us "and subject to action," not about the eternal, that is, what always happens in some way or by chance. We deliberate about what is related to ends, moreover, not ends: we set down the end (e.g., health or a good political order) and deliberate about how to bring it about most easily and nobly, down to the first step. Deliberation concerns "actions that happen through one's own doing" "for the sake of something else" and does not concern the facts, which belong to sense perception. What is chosen is "deliberative longing for things that are up to us."

Wish is concerned with the end. But is it wish for what is good or for what appears good? After discussion, Aristotle concludes that wish's object in the simple and true sense is the good and, for each, what appears good to him.[19] For the mature one, the wished for object is what is truly good, just as (for the base) it is what merely appears good—for those with good bodies, for example, the truly healthy, bitter, or sweet appear so, but not for the sick. The mature man judges correctly: in each case what is true appears to him, as if he were a rule or measure. He sees truly the noble and pleasant things peculiar to each habit, while the many are deceived by pleasure.[20]

"The activities of the virtues" concern what we choose, so virtue and vice, acting and not acting nobly, are up to us: our actions (and corruption) are voluntary. We notice too that legislators punish the corrupt and honor and exhort us to the noble. They do this for what is voluntary; they do not, for example, persuade us not to feel heat or hunger. Furthermore, ignorance that depends on one—drunkenness or ignorance of laws, say—is punished. Loose livers who do not take care cause their own injustice or licentiousness. It was at least possible at the beginning for them not to be this way, even if this is no longer possible.

But what of ends? Say someone is ignorant of the (true) end. He is not born knowing it, lacks "natural goodness in the true and complete sense," and what is bad appears good to him. Indeed, then, neither virtue nor vice seems voluntary. Still, the actions are voluntary and traceable to one, whether or not we also cause our habits and (thus) what we set down as our end. We have authoritative control over our actions from the beginning to the end and of our habits from the beginning, for habits were once in our power to use this way or that.

Aristotle discusses the voluntary again as part of his discussion of justice in Book V. He summarizes his basic argument, as it relates to criminal acts. Voluntary action is "whatever act is up to someone and is performed knowingly, not in ignorance of either the one acted on, the means used, or that for the sake of which he acts" (*Ethics* 1135a24–26). (Moreover, no one suffers injustice voluntarily.)

Discussion: The Voluntary

Aristotle's discussion of what is voluntary analyzes the phenomenon's ordinary elements: it is not based on odd examples or fancy theories of the will. His view therefore corrects contemporary claims that may excuse criminal acts as somehow involuntary or necessitated beyond the perpetrator's control.

As with the other ethical phenomena that he discusses, he makes evident the topic's central features and perplexities—what the phenomenon is that later accounts often take for granted. He situates his understanding within what is visible about human choice: he does not separate free action from what satisfies longings and desires. The choice of what relates to virtuous action therefore connects what is voluntary to practical reason rather than to universal law-giving. (This is not to say that many of the actions one could criticize or approve might not be similar or identical from these standpoints.)[21]

The Virtues and the Passions

Chapter 6 of Book III of the *Ethics* begins Aristotle's discussion of the first ten ethical virtues, which continues through Book IV. Together with justice and friendship, Aristotle presents his discussion of the virtues as comprehensive.

Each virtue he discusses is a mean between an excess and a deficiency, and each involves choosing for the right reason, at the right time, in the right way, and with the right people. The end of virtue is the noble, choiceworthy for its own sake. In each case, someone with the virtue that pertains to a given thing uses or enjoys that thing best. As I have said, one reason ethical virtue is happiness is because virtue means properly enjoying the good things for which we strive and properly satisfying our passions. The measured choosing of ugly, unattractive, or indifferent things is not happiness.

To understand the virtues one must understand the passions, because many virtues concern the passions, and certain passions are themselves middles or means. Aristotle's most extensive discussion of them occurs in the *Rhetoric*'s second book where he turns to the passions to which the rhetorician might appeal. In forensic rhetoric in particular one should try to render the judge "of a certain sort" (*Rhetoric* 1377b25).

The central point is that things appear differently, or different in magnitude, to the angry and gentle, to friends and those who hate one, and so on. Aristotle's discussion includes passions that we can treat virtuously; others, such as shame and righteous indignation, that are not as such subjects of virtuous choice; and still others, such as pity or being emulous, that might be but are not among those he discusses that way. Passions are "those things on account of which people, undergoing a change, differ in the judgments they make, things that pain and pleasure accompany, such as anger" (*Rhetoric* 1378a21–23). And "what pertains to each" "must be divided into three"—how, for example, the angry are disposed, to whom, and at what sorts of things. One needs to grasp all three in order to foster anger. (That is, the rhetorician's job now being discussed is to foster the passion.) Aristotle then goes through various "propositions."[22]

I give some of his examples and discuss much of his analysis here. Anger is a "longing, accompanied by pain, for manifest vengeance on account of a manifest slight against oneself" or those in one's circle by someone inappropriate (*Rhetoric* 1378a31–32). Anger is at an individual, with the pleasure of hoped for or imagined vengeance. Slights treat something as worth nothing and actualize the opinion that something is worth nothing. To slight is to be contemptuous: a lack of respect is a mark of contempt, as is spitefully impeding someone else's wishes, or arrogantly, for pleasure and a feeling of superiority, saying what shames another and dishonors him. Those who desire something and do not succeed are especially angry with those who slight their circumstances "for each has the path paved for his own anger by the passion that is present" (*Rhetoric* 1379a21–2). And people are also angered by those who speak badly of things they take especially seriously—for example, those who are ambitious in philosophy if someone speaks badly of it.[23] (This need not indicate but does not preclude that genuine philosophers are ambitious or honor-seeking in it.) Aristotle goes through his examples tellingly, even showing us why we become angry at the bearers of bad news—they pay it no heed that they cause us pain—or those who ignore our needs—their neglect or inattention slights us. And people are angry at irony, which is a mark of contempt, and when slighted in front of those they honor. Speakers should (when relevant) make listeners angry and show their opponents are responsible for what angers people.

Fear is "a certain pain or perturbation arising from an imagining of an impending bad [thing]" (*Rhetoric* 1382a25). It is of close at hand harms with the power to bring great destruction or pain (hence, not all bad things).[24] These include signs that what is dangerous is drawing near—for example, unjust power or anger. For the many it is frightening to be subject to another, to those done injustice, rivals, and the stronger and ironic. Frightening things elicit pity when they happen to others, and "those who do suppose that they might suffer something are afraid," but they also have some hope of salvation, hence they deliberate (*Rhetoric* 1382b34). Confidence is the contrary of fear, and what inspires it is "the contrary of frightening." People are confident who have successfully concluded matters; or if they have escaped from many terrible things; or if they are preeminent in things that frighten others; or if they have not committed injustice; or if their things relating to the gods are on the whole beautiful regarding signs and oracles. The divine "is thought" to assist victims of injustice.[25] Again, the rhetorical purpose of understanding the passions is to arouse in judges the relevant passion. As human they are not neutral.

Discussion: The Passions

It is important to note that as Aristotle presents the passions they are not simply internal, let alone reducible to chemical or physical matter. One cannot understand them if one does not see that they are always outward or that their activity and meaning always belong together with the goods they seek or harms from which they flee, and with the regime and guiding principle that limit and validate these goods and passions.[26] As Aristotle says, each has the path paved for his anger by the passion that is present. Our passions and the habits that direct them always first experience things in a certain way—as fearful, say, and what will or will not bring us safety. Or: as slanderous. Or: as shameful. Or: as commanded legally (i.e., as just). Goods, moreover, are never apart from the soul or body, for their meaning and desirability (even when they are "external") approach us in light of our passions, how they can be noble, our way of life, and our necessities. This meaningful approach is connected to the fact that speech and persuasion can influence their pursuit and even their enjoyment, through rhetoric, habituation, and philosophy. The passions are always outward and immersed in goods things, which are themselves always experienced this way or that: one therefore chooses or strives for them in a certain way. Moreover, matters are not meaningful merely as a particular passion and its object reflect each other. In fear, for example, we not only see what is fearsome, but seek safety; in anger we are not only angry with someone, but try to take revenge. There is always a broad intelligibility through speech that belongs together with the experience of passions and the goods to which they are first oriented. The passions, goods, and virtuous or noble choice comprise a whole from the beginning but variable wholes in terms of the trust connected to different regimes and necessities. We then analytically, and in ordinary action, divide this into passions, goods, and practical reason (or deliberation) and, incorrectly, tend to abstract pleasures from the activities they complete. This whole is easy to overlook, given today's science and our view of desires. But it is a crucial basic fact that today's analyses or even ordinary discussions miss. Longing and speaking are inseparable from what they are for, and what they are for is inseparable from them. Theoretical searching observes this but is itself never simply outside it.

The Virtues

Of the virtues,[27] Aristotle discusses courage most extensively, to differentiate it from its five likenesses, such as animal courage and legally demanded courage whose actions seem similar to what stems from courage as such.[28] Actions are courageous if reasonably chosen "for the sake of the noble, for this is the end of virtue" (*Ethics* 1115b12–13). "Courage that arises through spiritedness appears to be the most natural if it includes choice and that for the sake of which it is" (*Ethics* 1117a4–6). Although courage is connected to spiritedness, Aristotle does not literally call courage governing, directing, or giving in to spiritedness in a measured way, as he does with moderation and desire.

Aristotle's account of courage, or courage itself, also differs from the other virtues because courage is a mean between both cowardice and fearlessness and cowardice and recklessness or excessive boldness. Courage is proper fear and proper confidence. The true home of courage is battle, and it is above all virtue with regard to death in battle. Courage also seems to differ from the other virtues because it deals with something unpleasant, fear, and risks the lives of those with the most to lose, the virtuous. It seems as well to be noble (in war) only because it serves fellow citizens but does not belong to one's own happiness. Yet perhaps this view overlooks the charm for some of action, of mastery, of victory, and of meeting the risks connected with these. Risk or danger may have an allure that merely overcoming fear does not. This allure differentiates courage or manliness as a mean between cowardice and fearlessness from courage (or proper confidence) as a mean between cowardice and recklessness. (Aristotle also suggests, in Book X, that to complete what accords with courage someone courageous needs power.)

Moderation or temperance concerns physical or sensual desire, especially for food and sex, and is a mean between insensibility—or, we might even say, asceticism—and licentiousness. Aristotle's discussion is a lucid exposition of this basic virtue, clearly recognizable today. His discussion is especially notable in finding insensibility, however rare, to be a vice. Asceticism is not as such a mark of excellence. Sensual desire might be limited by pursuit of greater goods than physical pleasure, but Aristotle does not make bodily purity as such one of these higher goods. Indeed, Aristotle restricts his discussions here to the ordinary range of goods and passions with which a virtue deals. Unlike Plato, he does not open desire beyond physical pleasure. Virtue is noble, but moderation is not connected to eros that is directed to, and reflects, combining with the beautiful simply.[29] Courage concerns fear and confidence, not quickness, speed, protection, or separation broadly.[30] Aristotle first examines the virtues (and what may be problematic about them) in their everyday field of action and allows us to validate his discussions through ordinary observation and discussion.[31]

Liberality or generosity concerns wealth, and the extremes of profligacy and stinginess concern both giving and taking. Liberality belongs to the Greek term for freedom generally and is the first virtue on Aristotle's list to depart from animal passions and goods. Although liberal actions are calibrated to one's own resources, liberality is also the first virtue to deal with what differentiates the wealthy or aristocratic from the common or to indicate that full ethical virtue (and, hence, happiness) is not possible for all or, indeed, is possible only for a few. It is also the first virtue to deal primarily with external goods rather than a central passion.

Magnificence (*megalopropreia*) concerns large expenditures for noble or beautiful actions, say, providing for part of a military force, providing for sacred embassies, or outfitting a dramatic chorus. "The magnificent one is like a knower, since he is able to contemplate what is fitting and spend great amounts suitably" (*Ethics* 1122a35–36).[32] The literal meaning of *megalopropreia*—"being greatly fitting"—points to the beautiful and noble. Our current philanthropy reminds us of magnificence. It is more general or democratic in its objects than is classic magnificence but less confined to the beautiful and more a product of economic competition.

Magnificence continues the ascent from the animal and usual, although there is a kind of magnificence appropriate to an ordinary degree of resources—those we each can spend on rare and beautiful events, a wedding, say. Its vices are vulgarity or ostentation of the Hollywood type, as well as cheapness.

Magnificence also involves dealings with the gods as, say, some modern philanthropy is directed to the church and its princes. Magnificence shows with special clarity the difference between Aristotle's virtues of character and modern moralism and virtue signaling, with its finger-wagging demands and joyless restrictions. For, as a virtue, it belongs to happiness, not to unattractive duty. Still, the public examples Aristotle uses also point forward both to the next virtue, greatness of soul, and to justice, and one can see how magnificence can be transformed to service or self-limitation simply. And one can also see the manner in which using great wealth for such public goals is a natural ground for religious philanthropy for reasons other than one's own beauty or nobility. Aristotle's public and domestic examples, however, indicate primarily how the fuller virtues implement our own elevation to the beautiful, to the appropriate and outstanding. Virtue does not stand outside its acts or instances as a more or less general goal but, rather, is active in them as an end or completeness.

The peak ethical virtue is greatness of soul or great pride, which concerns great honors. Honor is "the greatest of the external goods" and is what we assign to gods and to the noblest men. Political power is among the things for which those who possess it wish to be honored.[33] The virtue of magnanimity is to believe correctly that one deserves great honors. This height, however, shows ethical virtue's dependence or lack of self-sufficiency, because it is others, either the great or the many, who award the honors or positions one's virtue deserves. The vices here are the typical political one of vainly believing you deserve honors or offices beyond your merits or the smallness of soul in which you seek less honor or office than you deserve—perhaps because, as with Socrates, Aristotle's example here, you have more in mind for yourself. In general, honor is an ornament of the virtues (while pleasure supervenes on or arises from it); that is, it enlivens or brings forward their beauty. If deserved, it recognizes the rare and the superior and elevates. The great-souled man is truthful, moreover (if ironic to the many), and possesses beautiful if useless things (which is a mark of self-sufficiency and of nobility). He longs to be honored for being outstanding, that is, for being truly outstanding, for dealing virtuously with significant goods. He strives to be honored for courage and liberality, say, but, beyond that, to be honored for magnificence and justice, or even for being outstanding per se, as is a god.

We may think of honor as acknowledged superiority or height, significant praise, high reputation, or admiration for what is singularly impressive. Aristotle's discussion does not claim that all wish to be honored only for what is truly high. Some, after all, expect to be honored merely because of great wealth. A central question, therefore, is that for which one is to be honored: Is it itself honorable or high, or, as today, does it often descend to mere celebrity? Those who most deserve honor are parents, the gods, and great benefactors, and the highest or most honorable matters are the fundamental, or "first," principles that the philosopher seeks to know. We may say that those who deserve honor, those with proper pride, are those who begin or deal with the true beginnings. In this sense, those who deserve honor generally (not just as one's own parents and benefactors) are those with the intellectual virtue that seeks to know the true or divine beginnings, or with the full ethical virtue that is the proper source of our actions. Moreover, political offices as what rule or begin are, as I said, also treated as honors.[34] In this sense what Aristotle has in mind with magnanimity is properly thinking that one deserves to rule, although this is not all he has in mind. Full political rule would allow one to use his ethical virtue fully because law and command deal with each good and passion that virtue enjoys.[35] Such complete rule, however, denies the honor of office to others, as we will see in the *Politics*.

We can also see that Aristotle's portrait caricatures some elements of greatness of soul, the elements of seeming to be above it all—the love of the beautiful and useless, the slow gait he describes, the unconcern with usual goods.[36] This subtly mocks the pride or pomposity often connected to good birth alone but also in its way caricatures pictures of Socratic or divine indifference. We can, however, connect this indifference to examples of rare actions of ethical virtue. Great pride points to a wish or claim to be self-sufficient, one's own beginning, as it were.

Aristotle's understanding of the political importance of courage, confidence, pride, honor, and (as we will see) proper anger corrects views that reduce all motives to desire and the satisfaction of interest. His discussion of revolution is especially telling in this regard. Tyrannies are destroyed for several reasons, among them, anger at being treated with contempt. And it is those who are reckless (and with military honors) who attack tyrants out of contempt for them, "for courage with power is recklessness" (*Politics* 1312a19).

From this peak, which completes (and encompasses) the other virtues, Aristotle turns to lesser virtues, some of which, together with their vices, hardly have names. These are ambition, or proper ambition (because "ambition" sounds as if it is the vice of its excess)—believing correctly that one deserves lesser honors rather than lacking ambition or having an excess of it; proper anger or "gentleness," rather than irascibility or excessive temper or softness or indifference; truthfulness, as opposed to boasting or irony, that is, the virtue of truth-telling socially, politically, or in company, as opposed to pretending to be more or less than you are; wit and tact, as opposed to buffoonery, boorishness, and crudeness, or dullness and dourness; and friendliness or friendship, as opposed to obsequiousness or surliness.

These virtues show again how Aristotle makes evident the root phenomena of human action and choice, not of morality seen narrowly. The virtues deal with the ordinary as well as the extraordinary passions and goods that still define human action. Anger (and indignation) is central to pursuing injustice and slights, to standing up for oneself and one's community. To turn the other cheek is no more a virtue than is constant irascibility. Similarly, proper ambition is important if one is to make the most of oneself and indicates again the link between virtue or character and happiness. The scope of virtue is the entire field of human work or endeavor in which measured action that stems from proper habits and understanding belong together.

This last group of virtues also raises several interesting questions. The final three point to friendship and (via truthfulness) intellectual virtue but in more ordinary communal or social settings, and lesser ambition and anger raise again the question of spiritedness. Indeed, boastfulness as truthfulness's excess, obsequiousness as friendliness's excess, and crudeness as wit's excess also point to spiritedness and its excess and deficiency at the same time that friendship, truthfulness, and wit point to philosophy in the city, or philosophers' relation to rulers. Philosophy is connected to but must therefore be differentiated from spending one's time merely playfully; philosophical friendship is connected to but must be differentiated from political friendship or like-mindedness; and truthfulness is connected to but must be differentiated from philosophy and the philosophers' irony.[37]

We should also note that of the two vices connected to each virtue, one is more vicious, namely, the one that shows most enslavement to the good or passion—fear, desire, wealth, honor, anger, social phenomena, or other men—with which a virtue deals. The man of noble virtue is oriented to goods but is free.[38]

Together with justice and friendship, Aristotle presents his group of virtues as comprehensive. From the Christian and modern point of view, however, this is unclear. For the Christian and some liberal-democratic virtues are missing in Aristotle's discussion: faith, hope, piety, charity, asceticism, humility, service, loyalty, responsibility, philanthropy, compassion, civility (niceness), industriousness, and toleration do not appear. Some of these could conceivably be accounted for by Aristotle's list or are democratic versions of his virtues. One might consider philanthropy and responsibility more democratically available instances of magnificence and magnanimity. And the virtues he discusses remain virtuous for us, even if democratically so. But others that are virtues for us—toleration and industriousness, for example—are not virtues in his descriptions. And still others are vices in his account: asceticism (or "insensitivity") and the humility that opposes or denigrates pride are examples. Moreover, some today have objects or fields of action that differ from what is contained in his discussion: Christian hope for a proper afterlife, as it affects courage, for example, or generalized "service" as differentiated from Aristotle's magnanimity, justice, or friendship. These differences make evident (although they do not as such explain or justify) the steps that we have taken from what Aristotle is clarifying.[39]

Chapter Three

Justice and Prudence

Justice: Law

Book V of the *Ethics* is an extensive discussion of justice and is central for understanding both the *Politics* and the *Ethics* itself.[1] Together with Plato's *Republic*, and more immediately or directly than the *Republic*, it brings to light what will always be justice's central elements. Aristotle's procedure here is the same as with other virtues: justice as a virtue is the disposition to do and long to do just things and to act justly. What prove to be the basic meanings of justice, however, are close but not identical: someone who is unjust may be one who grasps, takes, or distributes too much or is a lawbreaker.[2]

One who grasps more is concerned with the goods for which we pray. We ought to pray that what is good simply is good for us, Aristotle tells us, and we ought to choose what is good for us. One who grasps more of what is good also grasps less of what is bad and, thus, an unequal amount. All lawful things, moreover, are "somehow just." What the "legislative science" defines is lawful, and the law pronounces on all things. It aims at the common advantage, for all, for the best, or for "those who have authority," in accord with virtue, or in another way. "We say that those things apt to produce and preserve happiness and its parts for the political community are in a manner just" (*Ethics* 1129b18–19). The law commands courageous, moderate, and gentle deeds and deeds of the other virtues too and does so correctly if it is "laid down correctly."

Legal justice is therefore "complete virtue" in relation to another person (and, therefore, is held to be the greatest virtue, more wondrous than the evening star and morning dawn). Justice in this sense is the whole of virtue but differs from virtue in its being: it is virtue in relation to others, not only to oneself and one's family. It involves something of every virtue, we may say, but differs from virtue in its being because it differs in relation or direction or, more tellingly, differs from true justice if the regime is inferior.[3]

Justice: Distribution

Justice, Aristotle continues in chapter 2, is also part of virtue (i.e., it is not only legality)—for example, grasping more, from wickedness, as differentiated from other corruption such as cowardice, which is unjust but does not grasp more. We use the same name for partial and complete justice because they have the same genus: both exercise their power in relation to what concerns another person. But one, legal injustice, pertains to all things; the other, to honor, money, or preservation. This second justice is part of justice as the lawful but is not all that is lawful. In particular, it involves the equal. In injustice, I, for example, take more honor than I deserve in relation to another, as opposed to vanity, a vice concerning honor in relation to myself. Legislative acts that concern education of the common are "productive of the whole of virtue"; in partial justice, however, education pertains to an individual, that by which one is a good man simply. Whether this education "belongs to" political science or to another science "must be determined later." For perhaps it is not the same thing in every case to be a good man and to be a good citizen.[4] In this way Aristotle suggests that although all cities are comprehensive, they do not all legislate with a view to virtuous citizens; that is, they are not all truly just.[5]

Partial justice has two forms: distributing honor, money, and what is divisible among those who share in the regime, whereby one can have equal and unequal parts; and corrective justice, for voluntary (market) and involuntary (criminal) transactions. Chapter 3 is a complex discussion of distribution, with a simple purpose: to clarify geometric proportion as an equal and a middle. More broadly, the proper principle when distributing goods such as ruling offices to those who seek them is equality and inequality in using them well: equal amounts to equals, and unequal amounts to unequals. Aristotle indicates the contributions to the city that deserve some amount of rule: freedom, wealth, good birth, and virtue. Democrats believe that freedom merits greater rule; oligarchs, wealth; and aristocrats, virtue.[6]

Discussion: Distribution

I will flesh out Aristotle's points about distributive justice with an example.[7] Consider a situation where there are two violins, a Stradivarius and a $100 violin made from plywood, and two violinists, a virtuoso and a novice. The obviously just distribution is that the virtuoso should have the Stradivarius to play. The various complications —what if in addition to the virtuoso and the novice another virtuoso arrives on the scene, what if the novice owns the Stradivarius, what if he has a vain view of his own skill—do not change the basic principle as such. But they do show its limits, or the need to modify the principle of distribution in accord with excellence with considerations of ownership, of scarcity, and of who is to judge excellence. These difficulties allow or require compromises among these criteria. One sees in Plato's *Republic* the immediate power of the principle of just distribution based on best use, for there goods are controlled by the philosophical rulers: the principle of just distribution whereby goods belong to those who can use them best and are distributed by those who can judge this best is one of the dialogue's guiding themes. In actual political life, however, the criteria under which goods and, especially, ruling positions are deserved are not simply commensurable, tend to be distributed among different classes (which sets them against each other), and involve distributing things such as ruling positions that are always scarce. This is visible in Aristotle's view of the just distribution of political rule, and many of these issues are the basis of Aristotle's more complete discussion in the *Politics*.

I should say more about the limits of proper distributive justice. If one were to distribute all goods in terms of excellent use one would need to violate ownership, at least whenever one could not reasonably allow the use of private goods in common. This would lead to fewer goods being produced, even with coercion: there is a discrepancy in all actual cases between best use, ownership, and production. This, together with the difference that Aristotle indicates between the good man and the good citizen, makes a perfect political community impossible in practice. Nonetheless, the principle of equal to equals and unequal to unequals according to excellence remains the fundamental principle of distribution.

Justice: Crime and Exchange

In corrective (or criminal) justice (chapter 4) we treat the persons involved as equal, and we try to restore equality among the things taken by those who unjustly gain. The difficulty is finding the balance between what the criminal takes and his punishment. Punishment intends to restore this balance. We do not punish someone who steals a Bentley by giving the victim the thief's jalopy. And the community intends to prevent and punish, so it is not merely a matter of individual balance. Moreover, we intend to treat all criminals and victims equally but do not always do this. Nonetheless, as with distributive justice, Aristotle presents here the evident and proper basis of justice: to treat victim and criminal as equal individuals before the law and to try to balance crime with punishment. Judges in these matters, or generally, wish, as it were, to be the just ensouled, mediators who try to secure the mean.

One might say that Aristotle downplays some of the harshness of criminal justice. But he does not ignore it. As we will see in the *Politics*, he indicates both the necessity of offices that punish and the difficulty with them. Offices concerned with punishing convicts and debtors, he says there, are hard to fill because they incur hostility. Nevertheless, one cannot have a community if one cannot have lawsuits and punishments and if punishments cannot be carried out.

Reciprocity (chapter 5) involves justice seen as proportion in voluntary exchange, the equalizing of differences so we can exchange different goods. Equalizing and exchange are central for community, and money is central in exchange. Money is the "exchangeable representative of needs" and makes things commensurable, "for there is no community if there is no exchange, or exchange if there is no equality, or equality if there is no commensurability" (*Ethics* 1133b17–18). Acting justly here means not cheating or stealing. In his view of exchange Aristotle points out the roots of economic exchange in equality and commensurability in markets. These roots have not changed, but the place of production, economic expansion, proper professions, and access to them has. I discuss this more fully when I discuss the *Politics*.

In sum, then, justice is a mean, for it is bound up with a middle term while injustice is bound up with extremes, but it is not a mean in the same way that the other virtues are means (because it involves others also). So this is "about justice and injustice—what the nature of each is," and "about the just and unjust generally" (*Ethics* 1134a15–16). As with other virtues, one can act unjustly—say, from passion—without being unjust.

We may advance our understanding of justice to this point by considering Aristotle's discussion in the *Rhetoric*. In Book I he distinguishes three kinds of rhetoric, and each involves speaker, subject, and addressee. Judicial rhetoric primarily judges the past: its end is the just and unjust. It is about "accusation and defense—from how many and what sorts the syllogisms [that make up the substance of the rhetoric] should be formed" (*Rhetoric* 1368b1). Doing injustice is doing harm voluntarily, contrary to particular (written) and common (unwritten and commonly agreed on) laws.

For the sake of what is injustice committed, with what disposition, and against whom? All that people do is necessarily (i.e., there is no other possibility) traceable to seven causes: chance, nature, force (these three are not due to oneself, and nature and force are necessary), habit, calculation (rational longing), spiritedness, and desire (irrational longing) (these four are caused by oneself).[8]

Aristotle then describes these seven causes further. What arises from chance has an indeterminate cause, does not arise for the sake of something, and is not always or for the most part so.[9] What arises from nature has its cause in itself, regularly, always, or for the most part turning out similarly. (The contrary to nature seems caused by chance.) What is done by calculation is held to be advantageous or conducive to advantage. Vengeance through spiritedness and what is done through desire appear pleasant, and the habitual (e.g., virtue) resides among these. And what is done through force is done by people contrary to their desire or calculation.

Why, then, do people act unjustly? In Book I, chapter 12, he suggests that people commit injustice for the sake of the goods and pleasures (such as money) he has discussed earlier (and which I discussed above.) How, next, are they disposed when they do so, and against whom? They act unjustly when they think they will go undetected, pay no penalty, or be punished less than they profit. They especially think this if they are skilled, experienced in action, and capable of speech, or have friends who are. Those go undetected who contrast with the crime (ugly adulterers, say) are unguarded, are only reproached, seem to act involuntarily, or are in need. Aristotle then discusses the kinds of people against whom one commits injustice, for example, those who are not on guard, or too ashamed to speak of the crime (e.g., women in the household who are treated arrogantly). An unjust act, he continues in chapter 14, is greater, the greater the injustice from which it stems, although one sometimes judges by actual harm, or when one sees that no vengeance can compensate or no legal trial is possible, or when we have bestial acts that proceed from forethought. All in all Aristotle offers a capacious discussion, noteworthy for its subtle breadth of human understanding. The ways to prevent injustice would be to guard, detect, and punish.

Discussion: The Simple and the Natural

Central to Aristotle's discussion of justice in chapters 6 and 7 of the *Ethics* (which presents his understanding of whether anything is just by nature or, instead, all justice is conventional) is what he means by the simple and the natural.[10] It is central because what is simply good and natural justice are the standards by which he evaluates the purpose and justice of political communities.

Something (e.g., what is good) simply, or the simple (or unqualified) version of it, is the chief, first, original, or basic version of it. It is what something is only, or altogether, or on its own, the thing (or its activity) as unmodified or unqualified, or "nothing but" what it is in its full or usual power. Something simple can therefore be the (most) universal or generic version of it, the most comprehensive version of it, the most excellent version of it, the most authoritative version of it, the truest version of it, the least complex or invariable version of it, or (even) the ordinary, usual, or paradigmatic version of it. The simple, therefore, can be what exists in every instance of something, or the ordinary instances of it, or the best, rarest, and most mature instances of it, or the version of it to which (all) others are related by, for example, its being their source or what they resemble.[11] What is simply white is universally or equally white in everything white. What is simply good and pleasant is what is good and pleasant for the virtuous, that is, for the excellent and rare, but not for everyone, for many may find pleasure in what lacks virtue. Political justice is justice simply, according to Aristotle, but is not what justice is everywhere. That is, it is justice's usual or ordinary subject, place, and occasion. Its other venues, the family, say, resemble or are analogous to it. Self-restraint simply refers to moderation and desire, not to self-restraint concerning, say, anger.[12]

Simple things need not always be natural, nor, it seems, need the natural always be simple or always be simple in the same way, that is, as excellent, universal, or usual. As I said, justice simply is political justice, and Aristotle treats natural justice in relation to political justice. Not all political justice is natural, however, and one wonders if natural justice is always political. What, say, of proper distribution that is not clearly political, such as the example of giving the best violin to the best violinist?

What, however, is the natural? The natural things are inherently self-moving or self-originating (and in this differ from what is artificial, the product of the arts) and self-directing to their completion and satisfaction (although sometimes subtly, as with human beings). In this sense, the natural, as self-directing, can be for and of what is universal, ordinary, or best in a species or individual. This self-moving and guiding occurs together with some material. The self-directing reaches its completion in most things (consider plants), but in man this completion also involves self-guiding (i.e., understanding the end and how to enact it) in order to be accomplished. Being complete is therefore not guaranteed, or even unusual, although the standard of completion (the nature of something as its full essence) is natural, that is, unmade by man.[13] The natural is inherently self-moving, but for man this inherent self-moving also involves variable self-directing or self-guiding because of choice and reason and because the guiding end needs complex materials to be completed. Because of this variation and complexity and because reaching our end requires others, natural justice is part of political justice. As its own guide, unmade by man, natural justice means what is most just or best, or the fullest combination of those two, and thus what guides or should guide everywhere. This guide also enables one to see broadly what is most just here and now, although knowing natural justice may be insufficient to give one the particular knowledge to achieve what is just here and now and may not always be explicitly necessary for this.

Natural justice is primarily a guide for distinctively human actions, for noble actions, however complex, to which we can direct ourselves rationally. But it also helps direct our inherent or animal motion and the attendant necessities of birth, death, and preservation. Natural justice guides us in a manner that is connected to our range of judgment and choice and, also, to our (merely) living motion. It thus involves political or just practices that are largely universal as well as excellent but that also must be particular, or conventionally made, because we cannot fully separate our animality from our freedom. Perhaps what Aristotle says about sacrifice and (market) weights and measures in the discussion of natural political justice that I soon explore is an example of this: there are practices that in some manner always exist (in cities) and are connected to original natural facts such as birth, death, and economic necessities (which are linked to our animality). Yet these practices can vary (be changeable, yet natural) because they always also need human making or convention to come into being. Even here there can be better conventions from the point of view of a naturally just regime, in the sense of a rare or virtuous regime. And the natural as guiding to possible noble completion or excellence may also mean an end that we cannot always fully observe, one where we combine the elements of politics—rule, holding offices, eligibility for offices, and so on—differently depending on the fullest justice (and virtue) we can reach in the circumstances and where we therefore also deal with our animality in more or less excellent ways. In this sense the natural as excellent is also variable.[14]

Justice: Natural Justice

The just simply, Aristotle claims in chapter 6, is the just in the political sense.[15] This requires sharing a common life among those who are free and equal, either proportionally or mathematically, with a view to being self-sufficient. It also requires law and common judgment about the just and unjust. As unjust, I distribute more of the simply good things to myself. Law should rule because otherwise we distribute more to ourselves and become tyrannical. A just ruler does not distribute more of the simply good to himself unless it is proportional; that is, he properly deserves it. He therefore receives (proper) honor and privilege or is a tyrant. There is, however, no simple injustice in relation to oneself and one's own things; no one chooses to harm himself. So there is also no political justice there: political justice exists "among those for whom law is natural, namely, those for whom there is equality in ruling and being ruled" (*Ethics* 1134b15–16). There is still more of the just in household management, although not equal to justice in the city.

Chapter 7 is Aristotle's complex discussion of natural justice and follows this discussion of political justice. As opposed to the natural, the politically conventional is what exists because we hold it to be so. We can make something be obligatory—for example, stopping at red lights rather than blue ones—only because we choose to. Yet why we require such a rule (and even why we choose to stop on red, not blue) depends on what is natural, as does the existence or force of law itself because of our ability and need to persuade and punish. Sacrificing to Brasidas, to use Aristotle's example, is conventional, but, as I indicated, perhaps sacrificing as such, or burying one's killed fellow citizens, or attempting to rescue the injured ones, or praying before battle, is partially natural because it belongs to necessities of birth, death, and fellow citizenship.[16]

What seems surprising is Aristotle's claim that natural justice is changeable. For, he says, the natural has the same power everywhere—fire burns the same here and in Persia—whereas what is conventional (e.g., whether to sacrifice to Brasidas rather than to another) makes no difference at the beginning but (only) once it is set down. Politics seems to be all conventional, he continues, yet (for us) there is something just by nature, as well as what is conventional.[17] The natural can be changeable, however, he claims, as we can become ambidextrous, even if by nature (i.e., the universal or usual situation with no intervention) the right hand is stronger. The human things change because regimes do, he concludes, but only the best regime accords with nature.

The significance of this discussion rests on the question of the degree to which political life can be guided by what is just as such, beyond human making. If not, everything is finally arbitrary, no standard exists by which we justly distribute and punish, and politics serves no natural end.

We may clarify Aristotle's discussion by considering the analysis of the natural and the simple. Each can be either what is universal, as white simply is universal, or best, as good things simply are good only for those who are good. One question is which (the universal, best, or ordinary) shows something's full (natural) power or full activity. The natural is also self-moving, self-producing, self-originating, or spontaneous, as the simple might not be. From this point of view, the natural can be changeable, because one can sometimes interrupt its motion or train what is not spontaneous (e.g., becoming ambidextrous), although with natural excellence (the power of the right hand) in mind. Aging and dying are natural because they are self-moving or not caused by us, but aging can be slowed and dying quickened in war. And full maturity—virtue—differs from these end points of our natural bodily motion and belongs to our (sometimes imperfect) self-direction or activity toward and within our naturally guided completion. In this sense, what is universal among human beings—for example, what we can each easily accomplish—is not always desirable. Moreover, it may belong to the natural to require conventional elements or surroundings to be fully what it is: the details of these elements may not matter naturally, or they may matter but vary by regimes. These facts accord with what Aristotle suggests (in *Ethics* X) differentiates us from (the bodiless) gods; thus, for example, our justice requires some sacrifices, but the details may not be significant.

We may combine these points for the present issue as follows. Politics is the simple or ordinary home of justice. This indicates the importance of law, which is vital in politics, but also the difference between justice and law, because we must choose laws and may sometimes or often choose poorly or unjustly. There is a single best regime by nature, one that is directed fully by our natural end, complete (ethical) virtue, and is therefore formed fully by natural justice. This regime, however, does not exist everywhere, or perhaps anywhere, in the flesh. Nor would attempting to implement it in inferior circumstances lead to the best result. Nonetheless, the best regime is the standard for evaluating the justice of other regimes that exist or that one might try to bring about.[18] Even the best regime will have changeable or conventional elements, however, as is true of other regimes. All have some conventional elements because of the particularities of time, place, people, and necessities while still fitting the regime.[19] Yet every regime will also have practices that are universal among all regimes—fire burns the same here as in Persia—but whose particular elements may differ among regimes. The elements of these practices are naturally excellent only when they fit the best regime: sacrificing to gods, not men who are treated as gods, say, or needing to trade fairly but with the precise measure of fair trade, or whether one sacrifices two sheep or one goat, say, indifferent within limits. So the regime that is naturally just is what brings about the best simply (and is the ground for the best here and now) and also meets the universal needs and requirements that any political community must meet, remembering that politics is the simple or ordinary home of justice and that for justice to be fully active it must be chosen, as is true of all virtue.

Aristotle also mentions the question of natural justice in the *Rhetoric* while discussing unjust and just acts in terms of particular and common laws.[20] Common law is the "law that accords with nature," something that all people divine. It is common justice and injustice by nature, even if there is no community or compact, such as what Antigone means by saying it is "a just thing, even though prohibited, to bury Polyneices." Of such unwritten laws, moreover, there are those "that refer to a certain preeminence in virtue and vice" to which, for example, dishonor and honor attach (e.g., gratefulness to benefactors) and also "those just things missing from the particular and written law" (e.g., the equity that is needed to correct law's speaking simply).[21] In equity one recognizes the differences among mistakes, injustice, and misfortune and shows "forgiveness in human affairs."

How may we understand this? We should remember, first, that the appeal to common law by nature is an appeal made rhetorically, in judicial situations, and need not as such equal Aristotle's own view of what is naturally just. Nonetheless, that one can make the appeal successfully is significant, and we must account for this in terms of the argument I am exploring. If we consider Aristotle's example and my earlier discussion, the point of the reference to Antigone is that burial is universal and comes from nature, as something that all divine, not from convention, although the specifics may vary, and we may conduct our actions incorrectly. This need not mean that the natural truth about justice is law-like—Aristotle here is discussing judicial rhetoric in terms of law—but that law may accord with it, as regimes may.[22]

Burial elevates the necessary to the noble or to the naturally divine. This is also true of what Aristotle says here about honor, if we take unwritten law also to refer to the law according to nature. It elevates the necessary, one's necessary dependence. (For parents are the central benefactors, as are teachers in a sense.) The variety of those who deserve honor, however, makes a simple rule about who deserves to be honored and when impossible to state, as becomes clear in Aristotle's discussion of friendship. Aristotle, after all, honors truth more than Plato. The mention of equity, moreover, reminds us that what is equitable cannot itself be stated as law. (Perhaps to be equitable is itself an unwritten commonality that may itself sometimes need to be ignored or disobeyed.) No law, not even the common or unwritten ones, could always be just, but some commands come close, speaking generally or usually, if not in all details. Moreover, the unwritten or equitable may involve what should not be punished even if prohibited or denounced by particular laws or practices.

In general, therefore, what is naturally just and fitting is changeable: circumstances vary, and what is best in the best circumstances may not be best here and now; even in the best circumstances choice and therefore variation must exist; law, when it exists even in the best regime, falls short of equity, given laws' breadth; and there are limits and therefore variation in the distribution of ruling offices even among the virtuous.[23] Still, natural justice is not without substance or invented by us. We are human, not divine or merely animal; that is, we are not only reasonable or only bodily.[24] Indeed, Aristotle concludes chapter 7 of the *Ethics* by referring to the relation of particular and universal—just acts to justice—without, however, tying this to his point concerning the best regime by nature. (As with other matters, he leaves the precise connection between the best and universal unclear.)

Justice: Equity

Aristotle proceeds to outline several other elements of justice, including what is voluntary, as discussed earlier. Just things exist among those who share in the simply good things and have an excess or deficiency of them. Simply good things may be good such that there is no excess, for example, "for the gods, perhaps."

In chapter 10 Aristotle discusses equity's relation to legal justice, which is also a topic in the *Rhetoric*. The equitable and the just are the same but not "simply the same." The equitable is superior because "it corrects the legally just." Law is general, but one cannot always speak correctly generally. The "nature of the thing" causes this. Equity corrects positing in terms of the general or universal case but not the exception—something the legislator would have done if he were present. It is not better than the just simply, but it is better than the error that arises when it is stated simply in law.[25]

The deficiencies of law that Aristotle points out are a basis to limit or dispute the view that "natural laws" are the full being of natural justice or could strictly determine proper action. All law is too general to match every case perfectly; equity and being equitable are correctives. This difficulty is inherent is what law is, however it is modified. Just government is formed constitutionally and looks to distribute rule or lawmaking properly and to produce a certain human character. Law as such is necessary but imperfect.

Aristotle concludes Book V by considering issues that concern injustice to oneself. One cannot be unjust to oneself voluntarily: a suicide does injustice to the city, and the "law does not command one to kill oneself, and what the law does not command, it forbids" (*Ethics* 1138a6–7). The just and unjust must involve more than one. Doing injustice is more base than suffering it because it stems from vice. If we see the soul as having parts, however, then one could "suffer something contrary to their respective longings," where the rational part of the soul is treated unjustly (*Ethics* 1138 b10).[26]

Prudence and Intellectual Virtue

Book VI concerns intellectual virtue, which has five varieties. I concentrate on prudence, which is central because it constitutes the knowledge that both virtue and the statesman require. The two questions that concern me primarily are the substance of prudence and its connection to today's understanding of politics and political choice. Intellectual virtue even more than ethical virtue constitutes happiness, as Aristotle indicated in the first book. He reminds us of this later in Book VI but does not develop the discussion of intellectual virtue's connection to happiness until Book X.

We posit the soul as having two parts, Aristotle begins Book VI: one contemplates beings that cannot be otherwise; the other, those that can. The soul "naturally relates" to these beings that differ in kind. The two parts are the theoretical and the deliberative or calculative. What, then, is the virtue related to the work of each? Sense perception, intellect, and longing are authoritative over action. Animal sense perception does not originate action, for action is choice, longing marked by deliberation. In mature choice, the longing and reasoning must be the same. In contemplating, thinking is true and false. In action, choice originates the action, but longing is for the sake of something: one longs to act well.

Aristotle begins chapter 3 "from a point further back," which proves to divide powers by which we attain truth. Science concerns what cannot be otherwise, what exists simply necessarily and therefore eternally or imperishably. Central in science are the beginnings or principles: science proceeds deductively or inductively from what one already recognizes. Universals are demonstrated by induction, and one teaches through them, or syllogistically. Science rests on trust in principles.

Action differs from making. The arts make, contrive, and contemplate how things that could or could not exist come into being, where their origin lies in the maker, not things that exist or come into being necessarily or by nature, "for these have their origin within themselves." An art "is a characteristic of making according to true reason" (*Ethics* 1140a10).[27]

Aristotle then turns to prudence and begins by "contemplating" what we say about it. We call prudent those such as Pericles who can deliberate nobly about good and advantageous things for themselves and for human beings. Prudence is neither a science nor an art: it deliberates but does not demonstrate, and it acts but does not make. Pleasure and pain can distort convictions about action's principles—that for the sake of which we choose—but this distortion does not happen with mathematical convictions. Prudence is a characteristic that follows reason about good and bad actions for a human being.[28] It is the virtue of the part of the soul that forms opinions: it is concerned with what can be otherwise. Intellect (*nous*) pertains to principles as such, and the "wise" person knows both what proceeds from the principles and the truth about them: he has intellect together with sciences.

Prudence or statesmanship is not what is most serious, because humans and what is good for us are not what is best in the cosmos, or the most divine natures. Aristotle brings up Thales and Anaxagoras, ostensibly to point to people's opinion that they are imprudent because they do not search for human goods or goods for themselves but, rather, consider the wonderful, demonic, and useless. The barely hidden issue, however, is whether their life—which must be chosen and is not given to us by necessity—is the best. Prudence aims at the best that we can attain through action, and it concerns particulars (which even those without prudence might know) and not only universals.[29]

In chapter 8 Aristotle continues his discussion of prudence. Statesmanship and prudence have the same habit, or characteristic, but different beings. One is concerned with the city, one with the individual.[30] Prudence concerned with the city divides between legislative science, which is architectonic, and the political, which is concerned with particular actions and deliberations, including specific decrees. Thus, there is prudence about oneself, household management, legislation, and the political. You can seek out your own good (and therefore can be considered prudent), but you can do this without household management or a regime. The young can know mathematics but lack the experience of particulars to be prudent or to know nature, whose principles come from experience, not abstraction (as with mathematics). Prudence concerns the ultimate particular, of which there is perception, not of the senses, but in the way that in mathematics the ultimate particular is a triangle. One must, for example, know not only that all heavy water is bad, but that this is heavy water, just as the intellect is concerned with defining limits.

Aristotle then further examines good deliberation, which differs from guessing and shrewdness but is correct thinking, although not an assertion, as opinion is. The bad person may deliberate correctly but attain something bad. But one may also hit on something good through a false syllogism or through long deliberation. Good deliberation "is correctness according to what is beneficial for the end" (*Ethics* 1142b32–33). Comprehension and prudence concern the same thing, but prudence is characterized by command. Judgment is what is correct about the equitable. We attribute judgment, comprehension, prudence, and intellect to the same people; each power "is concerned with things ultimate and particular" (*Ethics* 1143a29).

Indeed, intellect grasps the first defining limits and ultimate particulars. That is, in demonstrations, it grasps the first defining limits and the minor premise. The ultimate particulars are the starting points of that for the sake of which one acts—the universals arise from these, and people are held to have intellect, judgment, and comprehension by nature. Hence, one should pay attention to the undemonstrated opinions and experiences of one old and wise.[31]

One might be perplexed about why to seek prudence or intellect. First, they are choiceworthy in themselves, as virtues of the soul. And they (wisdom is the example) produce something: happiness as possessed and active (as health produces health).[32] And they (prudence is the example) complete the relevant work: "virtue makes the target correct, prudence the things in relation to the target" (*Ethics* 1144a8–9). Hitting a target whose nobility is chosen virtuously is clever, but while prudence needs cleverness, this eye of the soul is not prudence without virtue.[33] The good end, the syllogism's starting point, does not appear to someone who is not good. (Corruptions distort this.) There may be natural characteristics akin to virtue (e.g., inclinations to courageous or moderate actions), but they are not authoritative virtue and could even be harmful without prudence. Socrates thus said correctly that there is no virtue without prudence but was incorrect to call all virtue a form of prudence.[34] Virtue accords with and is accompanied by correct reason. With the virtues in reference to which one is good simply, to have one—prudence—is to have them all. (This need not and does not mean that prudence causes the virtues as opposed to necessarily accompanying them.)

Statesmanship and prudence rule over much but do not rule over the gods, wisdom, or the soul's better part, as medicine does not rule health. In these areas prudence may be like a household steward—in a sense sovereign, not as master over all, but as furnishing leisure to the master so that undistracted by necessity he may act nobly. In this sense prudence would be a steward to wisdom and furnish leisure (and other conditions?) to do its work, restraining and disciplining the passions.[35] Virtue makes one (act on) the end, prudence the things related to it.

Discussion: Prudence

What connects prudence and longing, and what does prudence see or consider as, or before, we choose? Prudence sees the action to be chosen once one longs to act virtuously because one has proper habits, or proper character. The seeing involved in prudence is a seeing of the appropriate, fitting, or measured action—the one that is an instance or example of courage, moderation, or other virtues. What prudence discovers is an action that belongs to, is part of, the virtue itself. The action is then chosen. When we remember that virtue is noble or beautiful we can recognize the likeness (not identity) to seeing the correct note or brush stroke. The virtuous action is not a mere means to an end that is separated from it but belongs to the completion, fulfillment, or activity of the virtue itself. Seeing virtuous actions is not neutral or independent but requires that one look in the right direction or notice what is happening or might happen in terms of its nobility rather than as a neutral perception (if such is possible), as an artist finds a new example or element of what is beautiful only by seeing and thinking in and from its direction, so that a line and a stanza are not means to the end of a beautiful poem so much as instances or parts of the whole. Habit or character, and thus proper longing, is crucial for ethical looking and seeing. The point is not just to control, but ultimately to experience the passions and goods correctly, that is, virtuously and then or concurrently to act prudently.

There is an implied syllogism in action (I seek to act moderately, this action is moderate, this action is to be chosen), but what is central is seeing that of the possible actions this is the moderate one. What then results is the choice and the action. Virtuous habits and practical reason belong together but differ: they are not related as two sides of the same coin, or as the concave and convex, but they are not separate matters that come together only incidentally. Rather, they cannot have their full being apart from each other.

Seeing in terms of or in the direction of the noble is difficult because of its many elements and subtleties, and prudence is more difficult and necessary and more a matter of considered deliberation (that is, sees less immediately), the broader and, especially, more political its field of action. For prudence or practical judgment is also political science; that is, it is often complex and holistic in terms of an entire city.[36]

Among the several other elements of deliberation, of which prudence is the virtue, cleverness is the most significant. One cannot be prudent without being clever, but the clever do not choose to be virtuous as virtuous. The merely clever will therefore not generally or regularly see what is virtuous because their longing is elsewhere. One cannot regularly see the beautiful (noble) possibilities if one does not see and seek to see them as such. Seeing in terms of what is intelligible as "virtuous" requires that one direct oneself steadily toward virtue as the end. In the broad sense of experience, to experience a dominant passion is, as we have seen, to experience matters in terms of that passion, to see things in the way they are, say, fearsome, satisfying, or honorable, and, for the virtuous, properly, fittingly, or nobly confidence inspiring, satisfying, or honorable. Virtue does not see goods and what satisfies longing neutrally and then calculate whether pursuing this one here and now is noble. Rather, from the beginning of a possible choice it sees and experiences what is to be chosen in terms of—as—its nobility or lack.

We can see this also if we recall my discussion of how virtue is an end or that for the sake of which we make choices. In production the end is separate from the action; in ethical virtue the end is in the activity. As I said, it is incorrect to think of the ethical end as a target somehow outside the activity, although Aristotle's mentions of targets may lead one to think this way.[37] Even here, however, the target belongs to and helps explain the other steps in the activity. An end is not as such a purpose, result, or stopping or finishing point. Rather, the end is fullness or completion, and something's proper activity is its being at work (being active) as its end. The activity can be more or less complete: virtuous action is the complete being at work. One may then consider in these terms an end to be a goal, purpose, target, or aim, even a result or stopping point. Ethical virtue is choosing and acting virtuously, which choosing (and acting) does not as such produce something external but properly enjoys the passions and goods with which it deals. Virtue may also have an outside result—when one gives to the right people at the right time for the right reason, not only the giving but the gift too occurs. Habit, or the settled characteristic by which one looks to and within the beautiful and measured, is central to virtue because the characteristics that help make up prudence (cleverness, judgment, comprehension) do not themselves have either the proper directedness or commanding choice that help comprise virtue. One cannot have prudence unless one has a virtuous character—and vice versa.[38]

Discussion: Political Prudence

Prudence or practical wisdom is often said to be what separates statesmen from ordinary political figures and to be lacking today. Aristotle's understanding of political prudence is, therefore, especially important for uncovering the basis of political prudence simply, its continuing relevance, and what in contemporary understanding limits it.

Statesmanship is, first, comprehensive.[39] It knows or seeks to know the political community's good. This makes it especially difficult to acquire or to practice because the particular acts to be considered are so complex. Yet it is also architectonic. The laws' generality can overcome the multiplicity of particularities and can be corrected by equity. The prudent standpoint from and to which the lawmaker looks is the community's justice, for justice is the universal virtue, whose true excellence is to be grasped especially by proper measure and proportion in distribution, correction, and exchange, the substance of justice as a single virtue, as appropriate to the community. This prudence requires that the legislator himself be directed toward virtue: cleverness and experience alone are insufficient but not negligible. But how extensive this virtue will or must be—how much it includes proper understanding of all goods with which the community deals, especially honor and great wealth—depends on the regime. It is especially when one considers a legislator as a founder or an architect of a constitution (or legislating in an aristocracy with full virtue as its end) that fuller understanding and prudence are required.[40]

Political prudence also involves knowledge of particular choices here and now, not only legal ones. What is the standpoint from which the statesman gains such knowledge? This standpoint requires looking and seeing in terms of justice. But it (and lawmaking too) also requires attention to necessities of the sort discussed when I considered natural justice and which Aristotle considers primarily in his *Politics* and *Rhetoric*. (The *Rhetoric* concerns among other matters the elements of persuasion in deliberations about what is advantageous for the city.) Presumably, meeting these necessities will fit the city's way of life, to the degree possible. This is one reason political prudence commands or controls arts with lesser goals, where the art itself is not an action that belongs to character. The statesman must be concerned with what is advantageous for his community.

The arts are in some ways a possession and activity of the soul. This is why they are intellectual virtues—even those whose skill is primarily physical or in the hands. Still, they are not higher than ethical virtue or prudence because they deal with narrow, bodily, ends and because we can have them and lack ethical virtue and the other intellectual virtues. (So, politically, artisans are often not citizens or are citizens chiefly in democracies.) The higher arts either deal with more complete bodily necessities than do other arts (e.g., medicine), are themselves more fully intellectual than others (e.g., architecture vs. carpentry), or help produce or affect (and therefore to a degree to know) elements of the soul such as passions (e.g., music). The other intellectual virtues are also excellences of the soul but are higher or more excellent than the arts because they—science, intellect, and wisdom—are directed to what is permanent or always effective, the (natural) beginnings or principles of what is not bodily or can be abstracted from it (the mathematical). Ethical virtue is a perfection of soul, and prudence is an intellectual virtue. Ethical virtue, however, is a perfection of soul that is oriented to dealing nobly with bodily passions and goods. Prudence sees what is fitting, virtuous, or noble in particular choices to enjoy such goods and experience such passions. In this way all the ethical virtues and prudence elevate us.

The higher ethical virtues concern the bodily goods—magnificent beauty, great honor—that are least attached to necessity. They are goods that are limited, sometimes very limited and exclusive, are individual (as, say, *my* honor), and depend on others politically who admire or grant them. Understanding and choosing what is just is significantly intellectual, through its implicit or explicit understanding of proportionate or equal distribution and of equity. The virtue of justice also deals with trade and crime, however, that is, with all the city's goods, comprehensively, including bodily ones. So in these ways we can see the rough ranking of intellectual and ethical virtues. Prudence is higher than the arts, but the statesman must understand and attend to bodily necessity.

Discussion: Prudence Today

The complexity of prudence does not obviate its importance. Is this importance not largely reduced by our sophisticated techniques, however, our separated political powers, our political parties, the importance of equal natural rights, and our view of family and citizenship? I discuss issues of family and citizenship in due course. Here I want to suggest the following. Happiness is virtue of character. Direction toward equal rights, freedom largely coordinated with satisfying desires, scientific economics, bureaucratic legalism, technological mastery of nature, and the vast size of modern countries do not change this. How but with prudent measuring of virtue and freedom could actions, including political actions, be directed or organized properly? Mechanisms of defense, economy, and medicine may vary (or be difficult to understand), but central ends and how to measure and adjust them do not. Political experience is now more difficult to attain than in places and times with more limited ruling classes, and economic and technological complexity make citizens' and statesmen's understanding of how to deal with public necessities of defense or economy more remote than previously. Success or failure in meeting these necessities, however, is still visible to all who look. Prudent measuring of laws and actions that seek to advance justice and happiness remains fundamental, and these goals (and what is contentious within them) remain accessible and guiding if sometimes obscured. Methods that seek to replace or limit prudent judgment are or prove to be unmoored and hence arbitrary, or too general and legalistic to be useful. Today's difficulty in advancing sensible political choice stems primarily from our improper understanding of justice and other virtues, of liberty, and of prudence. It is not that these ends and practices are otiose.

The *Ethics* continues in Books VII–X with discussions of self-restraint, friendship, and intellectual virtue. I have examined Aristotle's view of pleasure in Books VII and X and will discuss the other subjects in due course. But I turn now from Aristotle's examination of justice and prudence to his discussion of politics. Indeed, he concludes the *Ethics* in Book X by beginning this turn. Is contemplating and understanding sufficient in virtue, Aristotle asks, or is doing and using key? Speech can make the free one, the lover of nobility, receptive to virtue but not the many. Not shame but fear rules them.

What comes from nature comes from "certain divine causes," for the fortunate. But speech needs a soul prepared by habit to feel delight nobly. This is hard if one is not reared under appropriate laws, and if they do not continue, so one becomes habituated. Law is speech that proceeds from prudence and intellect, but correct ordering requires strength too.

In most cities the need for appropriate laws is ignored, but it is excellent when common care is correct. Otherwise, one should care for one's own offspring and friends or become a skilled legislator. Care for individuals is most precise, but this too is best if, for example, a trainer knows what applies to all and also to particular types. With experience and not science one could exercise "noble care" for an individual. Still, one needs the universal to become a skilled knower in art or contemplation.

So how might one become a legislator? From statesmen? Other arts' practitioners teach. But statesmen do not (or cannot) teach friends or others. One needs experience too. Sophists are far from teaching statesmanship: they think it equals rhetoric or that they can just pick out and assemble the best laws. But comprehending which these are is key. You need (as in music) correctly to judge the works, what completes them, and which are harmonious with each other.[41] Treatises are not enough: they help those (such as physicians) already experienced.

Collections of laws and regimes would help those "capable of contemplating and judging what is noble"; others would perhaps gain greater comprehension.

Hitherto undiscovered is what "pertains to legislation." So Aristotle will investigate this and what concerns the regime in general to complete "to the extent of our power" the "philosophy concerning human affairs." He then mentions all, roughly, of the *Politics* other than *Politics* I.

Part Two

Politics

Chapter Four

The City and Its Necessities

We turn now to Aristotle's *Politics*. As with the *Ethics*, I will consider how the *Politics* uncovers the central political phenomena on which later discussions rest and to which all political activity must attend.[1]

Aristotle begins Book I by claiming that the political community aims at the most authoritative good and that a political ruler or king differs from a slave master or household manager. What is central is form, not how many are ruled. He will proceed, he says, by following his usual path, namely, by dividing compounds into parts. One tries first to observe things "as they develop naturally from the beginning" (*Politics* 1252a25).

One sees first male and female for generation, as well as slaves. These make up the household, "constituted by nature for the needs of daily life." The first community of more than one household is the village. These (and nations) are ruled by kings, who stem from the household's eldest, so we also assert that gods are ruled by kings, just as we assimilate their looks and lives to ours.[2] The city is the "complete community" of several villages, sufficient for living and for living well. The city is thus by nature, for it is the end of these first communities and nature is an end; that is, it is what each is when it reaches its completion. The end, moreover, is what is best, for self-sufficiency is an end and what is best. So man is by nature a political animal, even more than bees are herd animals, for nature does nothing uselessly, and we have speech. Voice belongs to other animals as a sign of the pleasure and pain they perceive, but we perceive good and bad and just and unjust and "reveal the advantageous and harmful and hence also the just and unjust" in speech (*Politics* 1253a14–15).

The city as a whole is prior to its parts, to the household, and to each of us. (Without the whole body, for example, there is no foot or hand, for things are defined by their work and power; without these they are something only ambiguously.) The impulse to the city is natural, and the first to organize one caused the greatest goods, for individuals are not self-sufficient, and man is the worst animal when separated from law, the "most unholy" without virtue.

I should bring out two points here. The first is that although we are naturally political, the city must be organized. It does not appear thoughtlessly or instinctively but remains something chosen and to some degree conventional. The second is that Aristotle does not begin from the individual, as do thinkers such as Hobbes and Locke. We are not naturally authoritative as individuals. Rather, the political community is from the beginning natural. An individual without a city is either a beast or a god. The philosopher too, who is most individual because most dedicated to matters of soul, is political.

In general, the next few chapters concern what is natural and what is conventional in "provisioning" (or getting goods) and begins by discussing slavery.[3] Artfully acquiring possessions (chapter 4) belongs to household management. Possessions are instruments for use and action, and slaves are needed for action, for using possessions as distinguished from producing them. A human being who belongs by nature wholly to another is a slave, a possession, an "animate" instrument for action. If instruments could carry out their jobs when commanded or in anticipation of being commanded, however, one would need neither subordinates nor slaves.

Are there natural slaves (for whom it is better and more just to be slaves), or is all slavery contrary to nature—by force and therefore unjust? Reason and observation show that ruling and being ruled are necessary and advantageous. When several things are organized in common, ruler and ruled become apparent in them, in nature as a whole, and in "beings with souls."

The soul rules the body as a master, Aristotle continues, and reason rules passion politically (or monarchically). This is advantageous for all, as are male over female (superior over inferior), humans over tame animals, and masters over slaves, who, when their work is only bodily, are as far removed as soul from body or human from beast—one who perceives reason but does not have it. Nature intends (but often fails) to differentiate the bodies of free and slave, the free being straight, useless in slave labors, and useful politically (in war or peace). If some surpassed others in body as do images of gods, everyone would claim that the others would deserve to be slaves.[4] This would be even more justifiable with the soul, but it is harder to see the soul's beauty. So by nature some are free, some slave, and it is just and advantageous for them to be enslaved.

Aristotle then turns to slavery by conquest. Is it right to say that an agreed on convention that conquests belong to conquerors is merely rule by force? The dispute is about justice. Those who say that slavery that results from war is just contradict themselves. For what if a war's origin is unjust? And what if those of highest birth are captured and sold? Barbarians, not these, are called slaves, and some are slaves by nature. Slave and master by (mere) force lack mutual advantage and friendship.

Mastery of slaves differs from political rule, which is over the free and equal (by nature), and household management is monarchy. Slave mastery concerns using (not acquiring) slaves; acquiring them justly is a form of war or hunting. Slaves may learn domestic service, and one may use a steward over slaves while devoting oneself "to political or philosophic activity."[5]

In chapter 8 Aristotle turns to possessions and provisioning generally.[6] Provisioning provides, and household management uses. Animals' ways of life differ in terms of sustenance, as do humans': we have (idle) nomads and their herds, hunters (including pirates), fishermen, birders, and farmers (the largest number) who cultivate, or a mixture. Nature gives possessions to all. Plants are for the sake of animals and they for our sake—for our food and clothes—if nature makes nothing that is incomplete. War too is in a sense a natural acquisitive art: warfare is naturally just if it is against the unwilling who are naturally to be ruled. One form of the art of acquisition belongs by nature to household management—to make available what is sufficient for a good life (i.e., not an unlimited amount). Experience and art, not nature, bring about the other type of provisioning (namely, moneymaking): with import and export, we need money for exchange, and exchange then produces more money. The end of any art has as such no limit: it is the means that are limited by the end. So too with provisioning: the end is possessions and money. There is a limit in household management's provisioning, however, namely, living well (i.e., virtuous use). Wealth in accord with nature is household management and the meeting of necessities that accords with this, while excess in money is connected to excess in satisfying desire, and even medical and military arts are made into forms of moneymaking.

Statesmanship uses humans but does not produce them; nature does, as it does stuff for food and weaving.[7] Provisioning from crops and animals is natural for everyone, but from exchange one takes from another. This (and, especially, using interest that makes money from exchange) "is the most contrary to nature of the forms of provisioning." Aristotle then discusses elements of provisioning proper (e.g., livestock and farming) that involve experience as well as "a free sort of study" and does so too for trade, moneylending, mining, and so on. He recounts the story of Thales's monopolizing olive presses because his astronomical studies informed him that it would be a good olive season and showed "that it is easy for philosophers to be rich if they wish, though that is not what they are serious about" (*Politics* 1259a17–18). Cities too resort to monopolies: Dionysius of Syracuse ordered a private monopolist to leave, as harmful to the city's affairs.[8]

Aristotle next considers paternal and marital "rule" of the others in the family who are free. The friendship of husband and wife is natural: we pair by nature even more than we form political associations; households are prior to and more necessary than cities, and producing offspring is common among animals. Humans live together for reproduction and also to meet necessities.

One rules one's wife politically and children as a king, for they are free. "The male is by nature more expert in leading than the female," although things can run counter to nature (*Politics* 1259b2). In most political rule ruler and ruled interchange and are naturally equal, with formalities and prerogatives designating or attached to rulers (and the male). Kingly rule over children is based on love and greater age. Parents feel affection for their children as their own and immediately, as Aristotle remarks in his discussion of friendship in the *Ethics*.

Aristotle turns next to the question of virtue and household management. Do slaves (and women and children) "have virtue or not"? Both ruler and ruled have virtue but differently: ruler and ruled differ in form, not degree. The soul has different virtues for its naturally ruling and ruled parts. The soul's deliberative part is not in slaves and is in children incompletely. It exists but is without authority in women.[9] Similarly, each has the virtues of character needed for his or her work. Rulers should have virtue of character completely because reason, the ruling element, is architectonic and the rulers' work is architectonic simply. Moderation and courage thus differ in women, men, and children. Moreover, their virtue is in relation to the regime, for the household and its parts are part of the political whole. Women, who are half of free persons, and children must "be educated looking to the regime" (*Politics* 1260b15–16).

Aristotle discusses the connection between modes of political and familial rule more fully in the *Ethics*' discussion of friendship than here. "All communities are like parts of the political community," which aims at advantage for all of life (*Ethics* 1160a8–9). The lesser communities are for the sake of only partial advantage. There are three forms of regime, kingship, aristocracy, and polity (or "timocracy," based on assessments), and their corrupt distortions, tyranny, oligarchy, and democracy. (I discuss these at length when I examine *Politics* III.) In the household, fathers' rule is like kingship, which looks to the ruled's benefit, and husband's rule is by merit (as in aristocracies), each ruling where they ought, not the man oligarchically in all or heiresses who rule because of wealth and power, not virtue. Timocracies are like the community of brothers, and democratic families are those in which all are equal, none rules, and each has license.[10]

Discussion: Necessity

Aristotle's discussion of politics centers on the regime and its possible direction to what is noble, to virtue. We will see this in the discussion of Book III. The significance of what the regime forms, the city's material, is also basic, however, and Aristotle brings forward its substance. It is easy to overlook this if one concentrates only on the form. It is also easy to believe incorrectly that the modern emphasis on economic necessity discovers phenomena that were hitherto overlooked.

The city's first task is to meet necessities: it is for life as well as for the good life. But we cannot altogether separate meeting necessities from using resources beautifully. Moreover, Aristotle claims in Book III that life has "some portion" of the beautiful, for life has in itself some "joy" and "natural sweetness." But with no limit set by a higher use, desire can be never-ending. The household concerns using goods, not merely accumulating them, and its central goal is to educate children in a certain way of life. In this light, some modes of accumulation are more natural than others.

The necessities that cities meet are not only economic. Protecting one's own in war and remaining free require military virtue but also the right kind of territory and weapons. Aristotle discusses this especially in his outline in Book VIII of the best regime. In laying out the city one would pray for, he tells us there, one ought to look to health, with exposure to the right winds and healthy water, "for the things we use most of and most often for the body are what contribute most to health," and look also to a territory's being beautifully conditioned for political and military activities (*Politics* 1330b12–13). Safety requires walls, especially now given "the discoveries of the present connected with missiles and machines for improved precision in sieges" (*Politics* 1331a1–2). One needs walls because it may be "that the preeminence of the attackers is greater than the virtue that is human and resident in a few" (*Politics* 1330b39–40). One should consider walls both militarily and for orderly appearance, for "just as the attackers care about the ways they can get the upper hand," the defenders too, although they have discovered some means of defense, need others to be sought and "philosophized about" (*Politics* 1331a15–17).

The necessity of our death is to be consecrated, moreover, and natural and unwritten law—that is, not only the conventions of this or that place—directs how we face this necessity. Priests belong to the city (not to a separate global order) and look to god or the gods. This is to say that some of our necessities are open to what is noble or divine in us. As Aristotle also says when he outlines the best regime in Book VII, abortion (if the number of children goes beyond the limit) ought to occur before perception and life. "What is holy and what is not will be defined by reference to perception and life" (*Politics* 1335b26–27).

However much necessity is limited in light of the whole or the higher, however, it always attempts to stand on its own, perhaps because it is unavoidable. Those who protect the city's freedom or produce its goods, arts, and wealth seek to rule. The existence that Aristotle discusses of licentiousness, of the lack of self-restraint, of adultery with or without eros, of making one's way by piracy and robbery, and of ignoring the divine are all grounded in the necessities of reproduction (population), wealth, and defense that every community must meet and in the power of "life" alone to break free from other or more complete human ends.

Because economic issues are fundamental politically, Aristotle discusses them at length, even though they are secondary to and organized to serve justice and other virtues, that is, what is noble, as it is more or less adequately understood.[11] The economic importance of the political community is clear, but to base politics solely on what is necessary narrows and reduces it. Household management concerns acquisition or "provisioning," but it is for the sake of proper use. The limit to provisioning, or the measure of sufficiency, is the use of possessions for a good life rather than seeing possessions or money as ends in themselves. We may also suggest that the point of Aristotle's discussion of Thales's monopoly is not only to emphasize the difference between more and less natural means of acquisition and provisioning or to indicate philosophers' superiority. For to monopolize is not unnatural if accumulating wealth is the only or dominant end. Rather, Aristotle's central point is to show the importance of limiting and directing acquisition and provisioning in terms of the end, or good life—virtue, ethical and intellectual.

If Aristotle has correctly clarified the basis of political life, then the noble—virtue and character—must reappear even in communities grounded on necessity, although there they will be secondary. This is clear, for example, in any political community's need for or anchor in religious ritual. It is true that here and later in the *Politics* Aristotle downplays this anchor. He even indicates that we assimilate the looks and lives of the gods to our own. But to downplay is not to ignore. He mentions priests in several places, including Book VII's outline of the best regime, and, as we saw, he discusses unwritten laws in the *Rhetoric* and sacrifice in his inquiry into natural justice. What is fair to say is that Aristotle looks at the natural phenomena at the basis of politics, including (some of) the natural ground of reverence. He does not recommend political practices solely because they are divine commands. In his upcoming discussion of Crete, for example, he does not treat its founder, Minos, as a god or as specially favored by Zeus: what is vital is the natural suitability of Crete's land. And one may even see his discussion of Thales in this way if one considers weather divinely caused.

It is easy to notice both similarities between our economic practices and what Aristotle discusses and dissimilarities because we support economic growth and entrepreneurial activity. To ground politics on meeting necessity as well as on equal rights, as we do, leads to the effort to advance economic growth and, therefore, to a different view of whether money that makes money is merely conventional. For capital is one of growth's engines. Moreover, the technological efforts that allow the widening of natural limits in transportation, communication, health, and much agriculture allow the expansion of means to the unlimited attention to its end (in this case, health and bodily pleasure) that every art seeks. Moreover, Aristotle points out the tendency to turn each art into a means to increase wealth—the military (our defense industries) and medicine (our health conglomerates). It is also true that connecting equal rights to growth, competition, and self-reliance leads to and requires certain virtues of character—industriousness and responsibility, as I have mentioned, and the continued importance of democratic versions of Aristotle's virtues. If the basis of political life is the noble as well as the necessary, even making necessity primary and turning it in the direction of economic growth still demands virtue, privately and publicly. Moreover, equal rights are linked to or express a reverence for human freedom. To secure them is not merely to advance necessity or economy at all costs. This is not to say, however, that to secure equal rights is also fully to secure or defend human excellence. The question becomes the degree to which what Aristotle suggests are the natural limits to the use of economic goods remains a guide even with the explosion of the means available to meet our necessities and other ends. And here I am suggesting that the human ends, the ethical and intellectual virtues he describes, remain fundamental. Moreover, as we will see, the connections between various democracies and the dominant activity (e.g., farming) with which needs are met remain important in understanding sensible government.

The first task of a city is to help meet necessities. But whose necessities? Which inhabitants of which villages? Cities—all political communities—are comprised of these people, not others. These are the ones we defend. Citizens are differentiated from aliens and foreigners. It is not the case, as with Locke and modern liberal democracies, that anyone can belong to the best or legitimate political community. Nations, as Aristotle sees it, are too large to be governed: they are too large for living well—"for judging the just things and distributing offices on the basis of merit" (*Ethics* 1326b15–16). Other communities are too small to be self-sufficient. Moreover, not every inhabitant of the city is or can become a citizen: in all the regimes that Aristotle discusses slaves and women are not citizens. Nor are laborers and artisans citizens in any but the most extreme democracies. Rather, it is *this* relatively small number, who are fundamentally equal and like-minded, who are the citizens. A friendship or like-mindedness ("fellow citizens," "fellow Americans"), grounded in spiritedness, is a necessary condition for a lasting political community.[12] The city may be more or less democratic or oligarchic, but these like-minded citizens produce and defend what is theirs. The proper number for a city, as Aristotle sees it, is the largest that is sufficient for life that can also live well. This is a number where citizens know each other's qualities and where generals can command a territory that is "readily surveyable."

It follows from this that Aristotle does not favor world empire. Democracies such as Athens institute other democracies and Sparta, other oligarchies. But Aristotle does not advocate empire's desirability. To rule over more, he tells us in Book VII, is not to be more active or more virtuously active. The city should be small. True activity is virtue, and aristocratic virtue requires ruling and being ruled in turn: a just community (and friendship) requires knowing the quality of rulers and possible rulers. Moreover, rule needs to be shared because of the claims of wealth and (military) freedom. (And intellectual virtue is in its way more active even than political virtue.)[13]

One may compare this modesty to our own regime, in which proper rule is limited by constitutional forms that protect equal rights, by federalism, and by private commercial enterprises with great scope. Responsibility as a virtue suggests that one exercises greater freedom or self-direction by taking on wider tasks for others as well as oneself, but this is properly limited by equal rights. This limit also supports the independence of other countries, although the possibilities of projection of force, and the scope of weaponry, make alliances desirable. Aristotle even indicates that if there is to be an overall Greek regime it should be one of virtue. Such an overall regime, and attention to advances in weaponry, may be needed to protect human excellence but do not as such advance it.

Aristotle does not support empire, but he also does not ground politics in the self-determination of national or ethnic groups. He tells us in Book III that the statesman should consider whether it is useful to have one or more nations in the city and if they should be alike, which suggests that nations as such do not deserve self-determination. Nor does he claim that any group is in every respect superior or that some ethnicities are made by nature to be slaves. Of the actual cities he will discuss in Book II, Carthage, which is not Greek, is inferior to none. Still, especially in his discussion of the best city, he makes his view clear that cold or northern nations are spirited and thus free but incapable of ruling others and relatively unlettered and that Asian nations "have souls endowed with art and thought" but lack spiritedness and so are ruled and enslaved (Ethics 1327b27–28). Greeks "share in both" and are well blended and hold the middle, although some Greek nations lean in one direction in relation to another. We may say that it is not a mixture of traditions, religion, or even language that comprises the characteristics of people ethnically but some combination (which clearly need not apply to each individual) of the desire, spiritedness, and reason that we all share.

Discussion: Slavery and the Status of Women

Aristotle's better regimes form cities where few of those that a city needs are citizens who govern. It is in democracies that the number of citizens grows. But what of his exclusion of women and acceptance of slavery?[14] Does this belong to the basic or natural standpoint of the city? Our difference from Aristotle economically and in the household is not merely a matter of economic growth. It is also strikingly visible in his discussion of slavery and women.

To the degree Aristotle believes slavery to have a natural defense, he pursues it by claiming that slaves have a lesser reason: his discussion of natural slavery points to the fully natural slave as one who is unable to govern himself reasonably and authoritatively but can obey commands. The natural slave is not or not only one who has no reason as is sometimes said—someone who is merely a body—for he is able to listen to what is prudent, even if not himself able to see what is prudent. He is said to lack the deliberative element, which children have incompletely (but which free children develop in due course). This would suggest obedience and response to chastisement, or childishness. This is not full reason but not its lack simply. Less reason than this would make slaves useless for most purposes. But it is unclear how many if any actual slaves lack the capacity for deliberation.

Aristotle's discussion of conquest, of freedom as a reward for slaves, and his mention of treating slaves differently as humans from how one treats them as slaves indicate his understanding that his defense of some slavery as natural is inadequate.[15] And it is clear that he understands that spiritedness revolts against slavery. In discussing slavery in the best regime, he says that farmers should be slaves—unspirited barbarians but not of a single stock if spirited ones. But one must see here—or precisely here—that Aristotle's discussion of slavery is not limited to the household in the usual city but that slavery will be practiced in his best regime. Slaves are necessary, he believes, if leisure is to exist for the noble, for politics and philosophy. Mastery over slaves is necessary for the noble, but it is not itself noble. We should also say that a possible insufficient spiritedness that could lead slaves not to assert their freedom may show why they become or remain enslaved but is not a reason to claim that they deserve to be enslaved and should not rule themselves.

One might ask why paid subordinates or paid servants in Aristotle's cities—or, at least, in his best regime—might not take the place of slaves, even in the absence of self-acting machines. Some artisans, he says, are "under a special sort of slavery," but, after all, they are not slaves. Aristotle claims that the growing size of cities points to an increasing number of democracies. Perhaps he feared that an expanding number of citizens, as paid subordinates might soon become, would lead to truncated nobility. Indeed, Aristotle's view connects freedom with complete virtue (not what he believes is the truncated virtue of the slave), although he recognizes that nature does not always meet what he claims is its intention of the good being born from the good. Slavery comes into being through war. It is an element of the harshness of political life, for to lose in war is to risk being enslaved. Much as Aristotle recognizes the link between virtue and the city, he is clear about its other root in necessity.

Aristotle does not afford equal citizenship to women and grounds his discussion on natural differences between women and men (just as he deals with natural differences among the young and old in passions, character, and appropriate ruling offices). These differences do not hold for every woman and every man, and Aristotle makes evident the possible dominance generally and not merely domestically of heiresses—but this is oligarchical, not aristocratic. Rule in the household is to be aristocratic, not in the sense of rotation of the virtuous, but of rule in the sphere where virtue is most shown. Men generally are stronger, have, in Aristotle's view, a more powerful or dominant deliberative element (are less emotional, as was once said), are less fearful or more courageous, and are less ashamed to admit, and therefore more prone to take action against, arrogance. And softness in what most can hold out against (e.g., excessive amusement) is, he claims, natural in females rather than males. Women, Aristotle says in Book II, are wholly useless in war.

These differences, even if one agrees with Aristotle about some or all of them, need not lead to unequal political authority, as they do in Aristotle, and in our democracy they do not. But they need to be recognized. Is he incorrect to think that women generally have distinctive versions of the virtues or even distinctive virtues? In a good regime the education of children and the activities of women are not strictly private, and Aristotle will soon criticize Spartan inattention to women's education. Children are central for the family and regime, so Aristotle attends to the conditions for reproduction at length (in his discussion of the best regime), with the goal being healthy children and balancing as much as possible the times for male and female fertility. Roughly eighteen is the proper age of marriage for women and thirty-seven for men. Eighteen, he claims, is already beyond the age of (excessive) eros. Adultery is never virtuous.

The central point, again, is that Aristotle brings out several natural differences between men and women generally, differences that must be accounted for, whatever the politics. To (come close to) completely overcoming these differences (or differences between young and old), one would (as in Plato's *Republic*) need to overcome bodily differences and, therefore, their relation to the soul, to the passions and intellectual virtue, and to choosing the correct political course prudently. The measured course and the power to choose it differ depending on differences in passions and the ability to allow prudence to be authoritative in directing choice. The different habituations of men and women would also need to be overcome. Whatever equal rights allow, we must still attend to these original differences. How, if at all, one can reconcile equal freedom or equal natural rights with the happiness of Aristotelian virtue and the prudence of his better regimes is an issue that I continue to discuss below.

What we may say about Book I on the whole, therefore, is that Aristotle clarifies the natural size of the city and its natural necessities and goal. It is also in this light that he discusses the importance of a territory that allows sufficient resources and proper defense. Whatever we claim about what technology makes possible for size, resources, and defense, or the difference between general statements about nations and particular statements about their members, Aristotle attends to and clarifies the basic tasks of any political community and its first ways of meeting these tasks. One may or must try in all political circumstances to imitate the city where like-mindedness, sufficiency of resources, ability to defend itself, and mutual understanding of abilities among fellow citizens exists, for these are the first and natural standpoint, always measured, however, by the regime and its relative excellence.

Discussion: Education

Although education is a or the fundamental task of the family, Aristotle does not discuss it concretely until he addresses the education of the young in Books VII and VIII, when he discusses the best regime.[16] I begin this presentation with his outline of the young's characteristics (and those of the old and those in their prime) in the *Rhetoric.* His discussion of characteristics generalizes. The young as young generally love honor and victory; love money least because they have not experienced want; are naive and trusting, not having observed much that is wicked and deceptive; are courageous, hopeful, and sensitive to shame, for they have been educated by the law alone and do not suppose other things can be noble; are great souled, that is, deem themselves deserving of great things, for not having experienced necessities they choose to do the noble; and believe that they know everything.[17] When the young are unjust it is from arrogance, not malice, and they are witty; wit is educated arrogance.[18] The character of the old is in most respects opposite this. Those in their prime are between the young and old in regard to their characters, not excessive in any direction, judging "to a greater degree" according to what is true, that is, neither trusting nor distrusting all, living according to both the noble and the advantageous, and being both moderate and courageous. They possess the beneficial things "in a measured and fitting manner." In all these cases the rhetorical point is that in speaking to people, one must see that they accept speeches "in a way that accords with their own character."

These characteristics are connected to Aristotle's examination of the education of the young in the best regime. Exercise is beneficial, especially for instilling habits that are useful militarily. And because "we are always fonder of the first things that we encounter," one should make what is illiberal, and comedy, lampoons, and foul speech, "foreign to the young."[19] Their play should imitate what they will later deal with seriously, for in educating one follows "nature's [temporal] dividing point." "For all art and education wish to supply what is lacking in nature" (*Politics* 1337a1-2).

The legislator must make the education of the young "his object above all," Aristotle begins Book VIII. One should educate with a view to each regime. "For the character in each regime is the usual safeguard of the regime and establishes it from the beginning"—a democratic character, a democratic regime, an oligarchic character, an oligarchic one (*Politics* 1337a10). "A better character is always the cause of a better regime" (*Politics* 1337a14–18). The city has a single end, so there must be the same education for all, public, not private. Each citizen must be seen as part of the city. People should be taught some useful things but for the free not so much as to become debased—such as labor for wages. And a share of some of the liberal sciences is suitable, but pursuing precision is harmful.

Letters and drawing are useful for life, gymnastics for courage. Music now is mostly for pleasure, but originally it was because "nature itself seeks . . . not only to occupy but also to be capable of being at leisure beautifully" (*Politics* 1337b30–32). Being at leisure is more an end than being occupied: this is the beginning of everything. We should not spend leisure at play, for this is mere relaxation from business, like sleep and strong drink. But being at leisure "is itself opined to have pleasure, happiness, and blessed living" (*Politics* 1338a2–3). One ought therefore to be educated for leisure spent in pastime, with studies that are for their own sake. "To seek everywhere utility is least fitting for the magnanimous and free" (*Politics* 1338b3–4).[20]

Aristotle then turns more concretely to gymnastic education and courage. Sparta turns out people who are too savage, but courage does not always accompany the most savage but rather those with "tamer and lion-like characters" (*Politics* 1338b19). The leading role must go to the beautiful, not the beastlike. (Courage is not the only virtue.) Aristotle then discusses appropriate exercises at various ages of youth. "One should not exert oneself with the mind and the body at the same time," since each "is naturally apt to produce opposite things" (*Politics* 1339a7–10).

Aristotle next discusses music (in the literal sense). Is music for relaxation, is it conducive to character, or does it contribute to a pastime and prudence? Learning is not play, for learning comes with "pain." Music is pleasant, so it is relaxing, as well as beautiful, as a pastime should be. But people "too often" take play and its pleasure as the end. Is music more honorable than this, contributing also to one's character and the soul? Yes: Those who listen to imitations experience similar passions, and virtue is connected to enjoying correctly. One should learn and become habituated to correctly judging and enjoying decent characters and beautiful actions.[21]

Aristotle's discussion of education then breaks off, as does the *Politics*, although the guidelines and substance of education, in political science and philosophy, are indicated in Aristotle's works as a whole. The basic point here is the priority and centrality of civic education, especially in good regimes. I discuss this more fully later.

Chapter Five

The Regime

Good Cities?

Book II is another beginning (as is Book III). It starts with Aristotle telling us that he is looking into which political community is "superior to all" for those capable of living "according to prayer" (*Politics* 1260b29–30). In Book II, he examines regimes in cities "said to be well arranged," and still others, largely devised intellectually.[1] In general, Aristotle's discussion here and in the succeeding books shows the practical caution or conservatism that is a twin of philosophical radicalism.

The "natural beginning" of the investigation is whether citizens should share everything, nothing, or only some things. Is the city of Plato's *Republic* the best regime? (Aristotle treats the *Republic* as if the city's practices described in and through Book V are meant to come about rather than a way to explore justice and the happiness of the soul.) Socrates's republic's sharing all is inconvenient, and having women be common to all "does not even follow from his arguments." Aristotle's criticisms here (which treat the *Republic* as concluding with the discussion of communism and ignore the discussion of philosophy) are meant to teach us about both the desirability and the limits of unity in a city and about the ordinary link between pleasure, virtue, and the naturalness of one's own. He therefore discusses the difficulties of love, arrogant behavior, and care of possessions that would arise because of communism. "Both a household and a city ought to be somehow one, but not in all" (*Politics* 1263b30). Each person's love of himself is natural. Cities come from those who differ in form, and it is "reciprocal equality" that preserves cities. The nature of a city is not to be a one as a household or person is: its self-sufficiency and goodness involve many people, and where men are all free and equal they should justly share in ruling. It is best for possessions to be held privately but for some of its use to be common or for one's friends. Moreover, Socrates "even destroys the guardians' happiness." But (as I indicated earlier) it is impossible for a city as a whole to be happy unless all or most of its parts are happy.[2]

While discussing Plato's *Laws* next, Aristotle claims that "all the discourses of Socrates are extraordinary; they are elegant, original, and searching" (*Politics* 1265a10–12).[3] Still, he criticizes the distribution of possessions in the *Laws*. And he treats the regime of the *Laws* as either a mixture of bad parts or as basically an oligarchy; he ignores the training in virtue that brings it closer to aristocracy.

In chapter 7 Aristotle turns to private persons, "philosophers and political rulers" who describe other forms. Aristotle first discusses Phaleas, who improperly supports equal possessions. This equality is not enough (to meet wants), for desire is insatiable, so whatever the subsidy given to people they want more: "the nature of desire is limitless" (*Politics* 1267b3–4). Aristotle's solution: arrange things so the naturally decent do not want more than others and the inferior are not treated unjustly and lack power to take more. Phaleas believes equality will relieve injustice. We are not unjust only from necessity, however, but from desiring excess, to feel pleasure, or to enjoy pleasure without pain. No one becomes a tyrant "in order not to be cold" (*Politics* 1267a14–15). Modest wealth may remedy injustice from necessity, but moderation and philosophy (whose pleasures do not need other people) remedy the other causes of injustice. Moreover, governments also need sufficient property to wage and avoid war.

Aristotle next considers Hippodamus, a pretentious intellectual, the first of those who had not run a city to discuss the best regime. Hippodamus divided cities into three (and did lay out Piraeus's grid). The main burden of Aristotle's discussion is to consider the fact that improvement in laws must be weighed against weakening the habit of obedience that arises from changing laws frequently, especially changes in the regime or hereditary laws. This difficulty distinguishes change in law from change in the arts. However, Aristotle does not deny, indeed, he emphasizes, the distinction between what is good and what is traditional (one's own): everyone seeks what is good, and what is traditional is sometimes silly and unintelligent. And written laws can indeed be faulty: they are universal, but actions are particular. Moreover, who is recommending a change, and in what regime, matters. Aristotle also criticizes Hippodamus's strict division into farming, artisan, and military classes while giving each class an equal share in government, because only the military will in fact rule.

In chapters 9 through 11 Aristotle discusses Sparta, Crete, and Carthage. "Concerning the regime of the Spartans and the Cretan regime, and indeed virtually all other regimes, there are two investigations: one, whether some aspect of the regime is beautiful or not with respect to the best arrangement; the other, whether it is opposed to the basic premise and the manner of the regime at hand" (*Politics* 1269a30). The Spartan difficulties are serfdom and "permissiveness toward their women." This leads to greed, and during "the Theban invasion they were not only wholly useless, like women in other cities, but they created more of an uproar than the enemy" (*Politics* 1269b35). Moreover, because of debts, the Spartan land, which could have supported 1,500 cavalry and 30,000 heavy infantry, came to support only 1,000 cavalry. The ephors (overseers) and elders were also badly arranged: the regime became too democratic. Nonetheless, "if a regime is going to be preserved all the parts of the city must wish it to exist and continue on the same basis" (*Politics* 1270b21–22). In general, as Plato said in the *Laws*, Spartan laws were all directed to only a part of virtue: military virtue. Spartans do not know how to live in leisure. The Cretan regime is like the Spartan one but less refined. The Cretans were Spartan colonists who followed the (Cretan) laws of the time and "even now" "assume that Minos was the first to institute this arrangement of laws" (*Politics* 1271b30). Minos established an empire over the area because Crete's island was "naturally suited for rule in Greece." Common meals are better arranged in Crete than in Sparta:

"the legislator has philosophized" about much related to a beneficial scantiness in food (*Politics* 1272a24).

Aristotle turns next to Carthage. It too is thought to be governed beautifully. It resembles Sparta and Crete but has no factions, and its version of ephors, the consuls of elders, and king are chosen on the basis of desert. But there are some deviations from the principles of aristocracy and polity toward oligarchy and democracy. "For whatever the authority holds to be honorable will necessarily be followed by the opinion of the other citizens" (*Politics* 1273a39–41). (This sentence is the center of Aristotle's political science.) "Where virtue is not honored above all," he continues, "there cannot be a securely aristocratic regime."

Solon and Lycurgus participated in government and also established laws and regimes. Solon added to Athens's oligarchic and aristocratic institutions and established the popular law courts (but elected, not selected by lot). He granted the populace only the necessary power of electing and reviewing rulers (for without this they would be slaves) but set things up so rulers would come from the distinguished and well-off. The expansion in the people's power came because of their "high thoughts" after the navy's victory in the Persian War.

Highlights of Aristotle's political understanding here are his caution or conservatism about change in the laws, his view of the importance of the military, his wish to keep material excess in check, and his rational or natural understanding of Minos, that is, of what some might consider his divine appointment. I have touched on some of these matters and will further discuss Aristotle's caution below.

Regimes

Book III is the *Politics*' fundamental book because it begins Aristotle's analysis of regimes, or what forms cities.[4] We will follow this book closely. He starts by again discussing the city's parts. The city is a composite whole, so we must inquire into its parts, namely, citizens. Citizens simply are those who rightly share in deliberation and adjudication, and this varies by regime. And, "to speak simply," a city "is a multitude of such people adequate for self-sufficiency in life." Cities are defined (primarily) not by place and population but by regime, as tragic and comic choruses differ yet may have the same members, or the same notes are scaled or formed differently. So whether a new regime's city should pay the old one's obligations is an issue. Moreover, the statesman should consider a city's size and whether it is useful to have one or more nations in it, and if they should be alike.

Aristotle next asks whether the virtue of a good man and a mature citizen is the same. The point is to suggest that virtue is the best regime's goal, that most cities and regimes fall short of this, that (as he develops the argument) the purposes of the other regimes are not random, and that any regime (including the best) should take the purposes of the various regimes into account and not only its own. As with a ship, the safety of the city or the regime (which is the community's form) is the common goal: although the precise excellences of the crew members differ, safety is their common purpose. The virtue of citizens differs by regimes, but "we assert" that a mature man is so through a single one—"complete virtue" (*Politics* 1276b33–34). Even in the best city, citizens have different works, so the virtue of a good man and a mature citizen is not simply the same. But will the virtue of a good man and a mature citizen be the same in some case? Is it, say, the ruler's virtue and prudence? Being able both to rule and to be ruled is praised. The tasks a good ruler needs to learn do not include the relatively slavish manual ones. Tasks performed by the ruled when they are free help one learn how to rule, as generals learn by being commanded. A mature citizen needs both, although the moderation, justice, and courage of ruler and ruled take different forms (as moderation and courage do in men and women). The virtues are common to ruler and ruled: it is prudence that the ruler has, rather than mere common opinion, for the ruled.

In chapter 5 Aristotle continues his discussion of the citizen. In the best city craftsmen are not citizens, but if they are, the virtue of rulers does not belong to every free citizen but only to those released from necessity. There is more than one regime and, therefore, more than one form of citizen—those in which craftsmen and laborers are citizens, the aristocratic in which honors are given merely to virtue and merit, and oligarchies in which the rich (and therefore some laborers) rule. The good man is the same as the mature citizen only in one city and only as the statesman who has or is capable of having authority by himself or with others "over the management of common cares."

In chapter 6 Aristotle investigates the regime more directly, "which and how many they are." "The regime is an arrangement [order] of the ruling offices of a city, chiefly the one that has authority over all" (*Politics* 1278b8–10). The authority is the government (governing body), and this is the regime. In democracies it is the people; and in oligarchies, the few. The highest—for humans individually and separately as well—is "to live beautifully." We also come together for life, which has some part of the beautiful, for life has in itself some "joy" and "natural sweetness" (*Politics* 1279b28–29). What are simply just are the regimes that look to the common advantage: this can also incidentally be to the rulers' advantage. What looks only to the rulers' advantage are deviations from the right form.

The regimes (chapter 7) depend first on whether one, few, or many are in authority. The first three rule for the common advantage—rule of one, kingship; of a few best or with a view to what is best for the city, aristocracy; and of the many who have warlike virtue and where the war-fighting part has authority, polity. (Not more than one or few will be vigorous about or outstanding in complete virtue.) The deviations are tyranny, oligarchy (rule for the advantage of the few rich), and democracy (rule for the poor's advantage).

In chapter 8 Aristotle expands his discussion of "what each of these regimes is." Perplexities are involved, "and it belongs to one philosophizing" "not only to look at action," "but to make clear the truth concerning each thing" (*Politics* 1279b12–15). The rule of few and many in oligarchies or democracies is incidental: that on account of which they differ is wealth and poverty; that is, the rule of the wealthy is oligarchy and of the poor, democracy. For, in fact, few are well-off, but all share in freedom.

In chapter 9 Aristotle discusses the oligarchic and democratic views of justice. All get hold of some of justice but not what it is authoritatively and simply. Justice is (said to be) equal and unequal, and it is but not in all. Some believe inequality in wealth means they are unequal generally, others that equality in freedom means equality generally. Wealth would be a sufficient distributive criterion (for rule) if cities were only for the sake of living, but they are not merely for this. And mere propinquity, doing business, and not committing injustice to each other do not make a city. Rather, a city is a community of households and families for living well, for the sake of "a complete and self-sufficient life" (*Politics* 1280b34–35). This is possible only if they live in one place and practice intermarriage: marriage, clans, festivals, and pastimes are for the sake of living well. They are the work of friendship, the choice to live life in common. The political community "is for the sake of beautiful actions" and living happily, not merely living together. Thus, those who contribute most to this have a greater part in the city than those who are equal to them in freedom or surpass them in birth or wealth but with less virtue.

In chapter 10 Aristotle asks what the authority ought to be. It is not just if the poor rule and divide up the rich's things, even if this is enacted "justly." This (mere force, like a tyrant) would destroy the city—similarly if the rich take what belongs to the poor. Should the decent (equitable) always rule, however, they would then be depriving all others of honors (offices). Should one rule? Still more would be deprived of honor. Should the law and no human rule? But this will in fact be oligarchic or democratic rule.[5]

In chapter 11 Aristotle turns to the multitude's claim to authority versus the best. Combined (not individually) they are, in certain cases, better than the excellent—as they better judge poets and music, each judging a part, each having a part of virtue and prudence. This might also be true of the share of rule they should have: they must have some, or they become dishonored and the city's enemies. Through Solon, they have choice of officials and audits but not rule, for together (and with their betters) they perceive sufficiently. But should we not give each choice to the knowledgeable, as physicians both cure and judge who has been cured? Yet, together, the multitude could judge (in elections) because with some arts the maker is not the best or only judge, as the household manager, who uses the house, judges it better than the builder, or the guest rather than the cook the meal. Still, why should people with inferior character have authority over greater matters than the decent? Yet it is the court, council, or populace (who, together, have the greater property assessment) who rule here, not the individual juror or council member. This makes clear that rightly laid down laws should be authoritative; one man should be authoritative only where the law must be imprecise. But which law and therefore which regime is best? For law will be bad or excellent, just or unjust, in accord with the correct regime.

Chapters 12 and 13 are the core of the *Politics* for they concern what should be equally and unequally distributed, politically, to whom. "In all sciences and arts the end is some good, and the chief and greatest is the most authoritative: this is the political capacity, and the political good is justice, the common advantage" (*Politics* 1282b14–18).

Justice "seems to everyone" to be some kind of equality, which agrees with philosophy's writings on ethics. But there is perplexity about of what the equality and inequality consists. This involves "political philosophy." Is it superiority in any good that is the criterion where offices must be distributed unequally? But, then, superiority in coloring (complexion) or height would bring advantage in just political rewards, which is plainly false. Better flutes should go to better flute players, not those who are inferior in the work but better in greater goods such as birth and looks, even proportionally.[6] "The preeminence should contribute something to the work" (*Politics* 1283a2–3). Moreover, every good is not comparable to every other as if enough greater height could outweigh lesser virtue. Political offices too are not reasonably disputed (and distributed) on the basis of every inequality.[7] The dispute concerns the things that constitute a city, so the well-born, free, and wealthy claim honor. A city needs free people, taxpayers, and "justice and military virtue." "Without the former there cannot be a city and without the latter it cannot be beautifully administered" (*Politics* 1283a22–23).

One may dispute about these inequalities for the city, but for the good life, education and virtue "above all" would have a just claim. For the city, being unequal in one respect does not mean one should be unequal in all: each has a just claim in a certain way but not simply. The rich have more common territory and keep agreements; the free and well-born have family virtue; and virtue has a just argument, for justice is communal virtue, from which other virtues follow. And the majority, taken together, are stronger, richer, "and better" than the few. When any regime is ruled by one of these the authoritative element is not disputed. But what if they are together in one city? If the virtuous are very few, can they administer the city? If the rich, will it be the one richest, or if the free, the one of best birth, or the one most virtuous? If the multitude claim justly to rule through strength, what if one or a few are strongest? So none of these defining principles for meriting rule is right. And the many may be wealthier or more virtuous as a whole. Perhaps what is right is the advantage of the whole city and of the citizens in common. What, however, if one or a few greatly surpass the others in virtue? Such a one who is "like a god among human beings" would suffer injustice in not ruling. He would be a law unto himself, but legislation is "for those who are equal in birth and capacity." "It would be ridiculous . . . if we attempted to legislate for them" (*Politics* 1284a12–14). Indeed, cities ostracize, and tyrants and democracies cut down the superior. This issue concerns even correct regimes. No chorus, for example, allows as a member one with a louder, more beautiful voice than the entire chorus. The legislator should organize matters so that ostracism is not necessary, but it may be—and some such corrective may be needed in decent regimes, although it is not simply just. Yet it is a perplexity: In the best regime, what does one do with one of outstanding virtue? One would neither ostracize nor rule over him. What is natural (like Zeus) is to make him perpetual king.

Aristotle thus turns to the varieties of kingship or monarchy both to clarify the place of virtue and to differentiate it from ordinary superiority. The two cases he examines at length are generalship and the form where one has authority over all matters. Is either advantageous? The first might arise in any regime, so the key question concerns kingship as a regime, and here the issue is, "is it more advantageous to be ruled by the best man or by the best laws?" (*Politics* 1286a9–10). Laws speak only of what is universal, so "it is foolish" in any art to rule in accord with "written rules." Yet this universal account ought to be present to the ruler, and because it has no passionate ingredient, law is superior to what contains it, the human soul. Still, one does deliberate more beautifully about particulars. So it is clear that the ruler must be a legislator, but laws must not be in authority when they deviate from what is right. Perhaps, then, all the people should deliberate, at least if there are a number who are both good men and good citizens. Aristocracy—likeness in virtue—is therefore preferable to kingship. Kingship begins when one is superior in virtue, but as many become alike in virtue they set up what is more communal. But if or when this becomes a corrupt oligarchy, which then concentrates greed into one tyrannical hand, the multitude becomes strong. Now "that cities have become even larger, it is perhaps no longer easy for any regime to arise other than a democracy" (*Politics* 1286b20–22).

Aristotle now (chapter 16) returns to the question of rule of a king versus rule of the best laws and conducts a dialectical discussion. Some say it is not natural for one person to rule where citizens are similar. In that case "justice and merit must necessarily be the same according to nature" (*Politics* 1287a12). They should "rule and be ruled by turns," and "this is already law." For the arrangement of ruling and being ruled is law (i.e., constitutional law). If some rule, they can protect the law. Moreover, the laws educate and set up judges for particulars, and the laws can be corrected. Law is "intellect without longing," rather than the "beast" of desire and spiritedness (*Politics* 1287a32). The law (as justice) is impartial. And custom is safer than human beings' rule or written law.[8] Indeed, monarchs use as co-rulers those who are similar and equal; that is, they do not rule by themselves. A kingship is apt where a multitude's nature supports one family of surpassing virtue, and an aristocracy is apt where a multitude can be ruled by a few persons with virtue. One person or family with preeminent virtue should have authority and not rule in turn or be ostracized. It is clear, then, that one would organize a city under an aristocracy or kingship in the same manner and by the same means that a man becomes excellent. The best regime is managed by the best, one person or family "or a multitude that is preeminent in virtue with respect to all the rest, of persons capable of being ruled and ruling with a view to the most choiceworthy way of life." "The virtue of a man and a citizen is necessarily the same in the best city."

So "it is evident that it is in the same manner and through the same things that a man becomes mature and that one might establish a city under an aristocracy or kingship" (*Politics* 1288a39–42). How, then, may the best regime naturally arise, and how may it be established?[9]

Discussion: Regimes

Aristotle understands the basis of politics to be the regime. The regime is the form, the ordering or organizing of the city's activities toward an end. This organizing is most evident in eligibility to hold and to select those who hold governing offices, but it is also evident in the existence of some offices themselves, as we see in the question of whether there should be offices that govern women and children. The end of human activity is an entire way of life, and in its completeness or fullness a virtuous way of life, and the way of life is most evident in the regime's dominant character. Providing necessities is (when possible) oriented to the end. A regime or form of government is not a mere structure but the active organizing and implementing of an end that is inseparable from the citizens' or rulers' use of goods and their opinion about how goods, especially the "honors" of rule, should be distributed and employed virtuously. The activity of the regime and its elements—in a good regime, just laws and action and education and training in virtue—is what it means to be working as an end, or working fully and completely, and it is this work that is paramount when one is considering conditions (such as territory and trade) that contribute to but are not elements of the end itself.

Aristotle's most extensive discussion of regimes is what we have just seen in the *Politics*. But he also discusses them in the *Ethics*' exploration of friendship and briefly but tellingly in chapter 8 of the first book of the *Rhetoric*. "The greatest and most authoritative consideration [in being persuasive] . . . is to grasp all the regimes" and the habits, legal customs, and what is advantageous to each. In the *Rhetoric* he describes regimes in terms of the ruling authority and its end: choice by lot, and freedom in democracy; offices distributed by assessments, and wealth in oligarchy; lawful education in aristocracy; and, in tyranny, protecting it. The advantageous is in relation to the end, and persuasion is connected to character and trust.[10] We trust and find most persuasive the character that is connected to the regime: these are linked to the end and to choice.

Appealing correctly to the character that dominates in a regime is, together with and sometimes beyond the content of the argument, the heart of rhetoric. We can see this clearly in famous examples of American rhetoric, Abraham Lincoln's Gettysburg Address most visibly or Ronald Reagan's D Day address of 1984, examples of epideictic rhetoric that remind listeners of the nobility of "government of the people, by the people, for the people," a reminder that is meant to inspire them to further effort. The appeal in Lincoln's First Inaugural to the mystic chords of memory (or in Churchill's finest hour speech to the British Empire's thousand-year future) is an appeal to the permanence of our place, to our friendship, together with a humbling before the divine that cannot in the end countenance slavery. The reclaimed or resuscitated friendship in Lincoln's Second Inaugural is oriented to a "just" peace and a lasting one, whose justice is grounded in equal rights and liberty. The rhetorical appeal beyond interest and necessity to the animating principle or "cause" and to the character of those who embody (and ennoble) it indicates the undying significance of the regime.

The significance of the regime politically should be evident in practice, but it is underestimated today for several reasons. The most visible is the basis and existence of our own regime, liberal democracy. The regime that serves equal rights, from Hobbes's *Leviathan* to Locke's *Second Treatise* and beyond (to Kant and Hegel), is said to be the one right regime or the one legitimate regime. This suggests among other things that liberal democracy claims to overcome or negate the essential conflict at politics' heart. Indeed, it is thought to be universally applicable or proper. This means that differences in population, education, territory, and resources are not relevant for finding and securing justice or are thought easy to overcome through economic growth and technology. Any people anywhere can constitute themselves properly.[11] Moreover, this claim is not eliminated—if anything, it is expanded—in socialism and communism. The factors that restrict the political possibility of the best regime—the need to accommodate a variety of claims to rule and the fact that the best simply differs from the best in the circumstances—are ignored or receive insufficient attention.

Despite this claim to universality, the factional basis of regimes cannot be disregarded or overcome completely if it is true. And, in fact, splits between rich and poor, elites and nonelites, and poorly and well educated persist (as does the spread of a kind of political equality). This is noticeable in the differences among political parties, in their rhetoric, in differences in professions, and in the choice of representatives.

The proclivity to ignore the way that a form of government fosters a way of life is also visible in the modern split between private and public. Government represents; it does not rule. It is meant to secure rights, not to form an entire character, simply advance the wealthy, or even (as in a classic democracy) treat each choice as freely available (but only to some) although not equally desirable. Most things are matters of private choice, so the place of common choice about common action in forming (and requiring) appropriate character and activities is easy for us to overlook. We are far from Aristotle's claim that what the law does not command it does not permit. Marx's claim about the withering away of the state is an extreme version of the disappearance of the political and its replacement by the private.[12]

Nonetheless, one can also see how liberal democracy, not to say socialism, is in its own way a form that in practice is directed toward the goal of a certain notion of happiness and a certain kind of human being. In our case it is happiness understood as the satisfaction of desire, or pleasure as the relief from unease, limited (only) by others who also enjoy equal rights. This also allows the choice of excellence, but in certain respects it makes it difficult. Liberal democracy emphasizes meeting necessity, satisfying desire, securing equal rights, and the concrete equalization of citizenship. It is similar to Aristotle's democracy in its breadth of citizenship (compared to his other regimes) and its emphasis on freedom. In Aristotle's understanding, however, individual freedom in extreme democracies becomes the freedom to do as you please but without equating all desires and pleasures as simply commensurable, as we do, although there is a (disparaged) tendency in his democracies in that direction.[13] And the expansion of citizenship in his democracies falls far short of ours, excluding women as they do, and practicing slavery. Furthermore, he does not justify expanding goods in a growing economy: use is still central in Aristotle's analysis, not acquisition.[14]

One can also see how liberal democracy remains a regime in Aristotle's sense by recognizing that to pursue one's desires or exercise one's equal rights successfully requires characteristically modern virtues—responsibility, toleration, industriousness, and civility. The decline of these modern virtues (and of modern versions of classical virtues) so that, say, toleration means unquestioning acceptance or even encouragement, and one's own responsibilities are to be met by others, is a decline in contemporary liberal democracy and a difficulty with it. This decline has many causes. Among them is not recognizing the true requirements of virtue or character in our way of life, the failure to understand the roots of liberty and its possible orientation to excellence, and a substituting of various forms of substantive equality for equal rights. The result is our growing (but not inevitable) combination of decreasingly few individual restrictions in many areas of private life combined with increasing restrictions on what it is publicly acceptable to say about the proper use of liberty and the true grounds of equality. What all this shows is that the dominant feature of our political life as of all political life is its being directed to forming a certain character and its being grounded on education and opinion about proper liberty and equality and education to support that opinion.

Still another modern element that seems to obviate or lessen the import of Aristotle's discussion of regimes is separation of powers. Again, we notice the novelty—and can largely question, understand, or improve on this novelty—from Aristotle's base. Aristotle prefers varied criteria for eligibility and selection for different offices in different regimes, most visibly, as we will see, in polities. The deliberative officials, magistrates, and jurors do not have different degrees of shared power that check each other. Rather, each has its own function. With proper arrangements the offices help to secure the fullest justice and prudence within the limits that necessity and the most powerful groups in the city allow. Our complexities of representation, judicial independence, and an executive who claims merely to execute and serve are best understood on the basis of—and as modifications of—laws, jurors, and magistrates who are meant to advance a way of life and to political positions seen as honors that recognize the contribution to the common good of the city's various free elements.

These deviations or occlusions from Aristotle's political practice are grounded in new theoretical understanding, much of which stresses—not altogether or obviously correctly—different elements of what he has already uncovered. Three elements that stand out are the modern emphasis on necessity, the further, related overemphasis on economic causality, and the later emphasis on facts such as ethnicity and territory.

Beginning evidently with Hobbes and before that with Machiavelli, the ground for understanding politics and justifying a legitimate regime is its direction to necessity—to moderating fear and to satisfying basic, universal desires. The fear of violent death is universal; other "goods" are only what happen to be desired. The universal human direction is to attempt to secure oneself against fear of violent death and to amass all the means required, all the power, to satisfy desire. This liberating of necessity and acquisition from limits of natural excellence or religious piety, and understanding political communities and institutions as "powers" in these terms, displaces human effort from the goal of completion (even if misunderstood) to restless striving for never to be achieved satisfaction. What is "good" becomes what enables limitless satisfaction of innumerable desires.[15] It is, of course, not possible altogether to ignore or denigrate the natural and differentiating striving that belongs to human activity in its excellence—in its completion—and the pride and honor connected to this. Nonetheless, later views of morality and ethics such as Kant's and Hegel's remain within this Hobbesian ambit, especially in their vaporizing, flattening (in morality), or bureaucratizing of honor and pride. The political elements of human life are submerged. And the notion of what is good merely as what satisfies desire is only a step or two from seeing what is good merely as a value.

To grasp and judge the import of these modern changes, we should see them in terms of the ethical (and intellectual) virtue and political honors that Aristotle examines and that they narrow, even while human assertion is broadened. Indeed, this viewpoint is also necessary to understand the honor that universal rights, respect, or dignity attempt to secure and the virtue and prudence that rational bureaucracy attempts to bring about. It is also necessary if one is to grasp modern political structures as in fact establishing and protecting a particular way of life.

One can also see the power of Aristotle's understanding of the regime as the basis of common life, whatever later changes exist, in his discussion of tyranny, as we will observe in his analysis of revolution. What Aristotle shows about the methods and goals of tyranny points out the still-fundamental elements of tyrannical methods of control: many of these methods are easier to apply now (e.g., the use of force) and some occasionally more difficult (e.g., the control of communication), but the basic methods do not change. The global scope of tyranny and especially its (false) justification through religion or science seem novel because they hide tyranny and justify it through indirection as not tyrannical, that is, by claiming merely to serve a faith or a rational cause.[16] In a sense they make tyranny worse because they seek to subsume the philosophical or divine counters to it: Marxist tyrannies are the obvious example of false philosophical grounding. This possibility too, however, can be accounted for in classical thought.[17]

How much these philosophical or religious principles are drivers rather than excuses for tyranny, or are even understood, may in many cases be doubted. But their danger as tyrannies, ethically and politically, and their methods have not changed substantially, although their scope has. The threat of a global or world tyranny exists, as does the closing of philosophical openness and seeking in regimes that believe they are based on universal philosophical or religious truth. The reasons such tyrannies are dangerous and unjust are already clear in Aristotle's defense of the city and its various claims to rule and in his (and Plato's) defense of the philosophical life and philosophical questioning. One might say, and Aristotle would hardly deny, that to meet this threat new measures must be taken, but the general outline—civic like-mindedness, ethical education, an appropriate liberal education that questions other thinkers and the excessive claims of faith—is already clear (and employed) in Aristotle's discussions. And the injustice of tyranny, why as such it and its methods are unjust, is clear in Aristotle, and this is the heart of the matter ethically and politically.

Just as Aristotle does not argue that each nation deserves its own city, he does not claim that there are necessary historical stages, although early governments are likely to be kingships. Our current claims that politics and justice are grounded in history, identity, ethnicity, and geography are among the reasons we do not notice the importance of regimes. But, as we see in Aristotle, these claims should be judged politically in terms of whether they offer proper understandings of happiness and justifiable reasons to participate in rule. This is to say that these claims can be reasonably, that is, universally, discussed. Justifications for power and views of human excellence and freedom that are supposedly grounded in or simply caused by history and identity can each be evaluated and understood in Aristotle's terms. As Aristotle reminds us, statesmen do not produce their material. Modern tyrannies—and perhaps to a degree even technologically driven liberal democracies—attempt to do just that. But they remain subject to reasonable standards of human powers, ends, and freedom and, one hopes, political choice that is guided by these standards. The importance of the regime and its purposes in understanding and improving political life may be occluded but cannot finally be denied. I discuss further in the next chapter the status of liberal democracy.

Chapter Six

Regimes

Stability and Change

The Variety of Regimes

Aristotle begins Book IV by reminding us that in complete arts only, one studies all that is relevant to the matter. Training, for example, studies what is advantageous for the naturally best body equipped with the most beautiful resources, for most bodies, and for fitness short of competition. With regimes the statesman needs to know both regimes and the varieties within them. "A regime is an arrangement [order] in cities about the offices, the manner in which they have been distributed, what the authority in the regime is, and what the end of the community is" (*Politics* 1289a15).

What regime, then, is most common and choiceworthy after aristocracy (which, like kingship, is organized on the basis of virtue furnished with resources)? Which should be chosen for which cities? How can we establish them, and what are the causes of their destruction and preservation in the "nature" of these things?[1]

More than one regime exists because the city has many parts: rich, poor, and in-between households; the armed and unarmed; among the well-off, the poor, and the people generally, farming, marketplace, business, and mechanical trades; among the eminent, differences in wealth, landed property, and horse raising and differences in family, virtue, and other aristocratic parts. So regimes—arrangements of offices—vary exactly in number in terms of the superiorities and differences among these parts. There are not two simple forms but deviations from well-blended harmony and from the best regime: when it is too tight and masterful, oligarchic; and too slack and soft, popularly ruled. Popular rule exists when the free (and poor) are in authority and oligarchy when the rich (and better born and few) are; incidentally, this is many and few.

As Aristotle said, various regimes arise because cities are composed of many parts. With animals, we grasp their species by first separating what every animal needs (e.g., sense organs) and if there are differences (e.g., a certain number of kinds of mouth, digestive traits, sense organs, and parts suited to produce motion), "the number of combinations will necessarily make up the number of kinds of animals" (because an animal cannot have more than one type of ear, etc.). When all the possible links of these have been taken together they will "make as many forms of the animal as there are combinations of necessary parts." It is the same way with regimes (Politics 1290b25–40).

Aristotle then lists again the parts of cities and now also their function: food, mechanical workers, arts (some for necessity, some for living nobly), marketplace/sales, the menial, and military/defense (to counter being enslaved). The military and what follows belong to soul, beyond necessity. He then adds what administers justice and deliberates (statesmanship), at least for the sake of the beautiful. A seventh part comprises the rich who perform public services, and an eighth part comprises the magistrates. The two key parts (because unlike the others, you cannot be both at once) are the rich and poor. The different forms of oligarchy and democracy are based on these.

In one democracy, all (including the rich) are equal and equally free, although the majority's opinion is authoritative. Aristotle then lists other democracies under law, one with a low assessment and one in which decrees and therefore demagogues are ascendant over law and which is therefore hardly a regime. Oligarchies too differ, from large assessments to tyrannical decrees. But in both cases character and the preceding regime may lead to more or less democratic or oligarchic rule than the regime that results from the laws: the transition from one regime to another is not immediate.

The forms of democracy differ by which parts share in government. When the farmers rule, for example, laws prevail, because they lack time for many assemblies. When the poor multitude can take time from private affairs, they, not the law, rule. Similarly with oligarchies: the number of people who have estates and can take time off leads to the dominance, or not, of law. Aristotle distinguishes four kinds of democracies and four oligarchies in these terms.

Aristocracy is a form based on virtue, in which good men and good citizens are the same and not only good relative to the regime. Regimes are also sometimes called aristocratic that, for example, have decent people, although virtue is not made a matter of common care. Polity is still another form: it mixes oligarchy and democracy.

Laws that are laid down beautifully and obeyed are two aspects of well-regulated cities. One can have well-enacted but disobeyed laws and laws that are obeyed but are only the best possible for those obeying them. One can mix democracy and oligarchy by taking a middle course (e.g., a middling property qualification), or elements from each (e.g., fines and/or payment for jurors). Such a regime is well mixed if you can call it either, and the regime is preserved because none of the parts wants a different one.

What regime and way of life is best for most, that is, not by a standard of virtue beyond the ordinary or an education that requires fortunate nature and resources? The *Ethics* beautifully said that a happy life accords with unimpeded virtue and that virtue is a mean. What is best (for most) would be a mean each can attain: a regime is the city's way of life. Moderate possession is best even with gifts of fortune because the measured and the mean are best. Extremes make it hard to follow reason: one becomes arrogant or servile and dishonest. Those with overabundant goods do not know how to be ruled; those with too little are humble and cannot rule. In between one is neither too eager to rule nor too eager to avoid it. The city made up of those most similar is made up of those in the middle. Best, then, is the political community that makes use of middling property, especially if it is more powerful than the rich and the poor or, at least, one of them.

It is free of faction and less likely than oligarchy or democracy to become tyrannical. The best legislators, such as Solon, are from this range too. Because the middle group is usually small, however, most cities are democracies or oligarchies, and they (e.g., Athens and Sparta) set up their own type of regime elsewhere. The ones closest to this middle are better and those farther away, worse.

In considering which regime is most advantageous for which cities, one must see that the part that wants the regime to stay in place must be stronger than the part that does not. Cities are made up of quality—freedom, wealth, education, and high birth—and quantity. Quality and quantity may be in different parts in the city, but the higher quantity may exceed in quantity by less than it falls short in quality. So one must judge them in relation to each other. Where the needy exceeds the proportion, democracy accords with nature, and the particular form of democracy would be based on the excess—farmers, artisans, and so on.[2] Where the well-off and notables' quality predominates more than it falls short in quantity one requires oligarchy, and, similarly, the particular form of oligarchy follows the predominant group. Moreover, the legislator ought to include and aim at the middle group—and where they predominate one could have a lasting polity. "In time from things falsely good there must result a true bad": the encroachment of the rich destroys government more than that of the poor (*Politics* 1297a10–11).

Both oligarchic and democratic devices exist in polities to make it more likely that one group rules: the devices are composed of ways to form the assembly, offices, and jury service and gymnastic training and arms. A polity should be made up only of those possessing heavy arms. Cavalry was key at first because "without organization the heavy armed element is useless" (*Politics* 1297b20–21).

Aristotle turns next to the parts of government. "When these are in a beautiful condition, the regime is necessarily in a beautiful condition" (*Politics* 1297b38–39). One part deliberates about common matters; the second concerns what offices there ought to be, with authority, and the third concerns judging. Deliberation (having authority) about war and peace, laws, confiscating possessions, and choosing and auditing officeholders belongs to all citizens (e.g., democracy) or some (e.g., oligarchy) in different ways on different matters and over or in accord with the laws. As for offices, they differ in number, scope of authority, length, and eligibility, and some who are elected (e.g., priests) are not political. "With all these one ought to be able to distinguish how many modes can exist and then fit the sorts of offices to the sorts of regimes for which they are advantageous" (*Politics* 1299a12–r14). Some offices involve all the citizens in an action (e.g., generals), and others deal with a part. Ruling offices are those that command.[3] One must also consider who appoints officials, from whom, and in what manner: some or all appoint, from some (by some standard, e.g., assessments) or all, by election or by lot. These vary by democracy, oligarchy, and polity and aristocratically inclined polity. Each power of an office involves that over which it has authority (e.g., revenues or defense). As for the judicial part, this is grasped "according to the same premise" (*Politics* 1300b14). Factional conflicts arise and revolutions happen when matters that concern the political courts (e.g., reviewing officials) are not "beautifully handled" (*Politics* 1300b38).

Discussion: Liberal Democracy

Aristotle's discussion is, together with the *Federalist*, the most telling analysis of the varieties of offices and qualifications for them. Politically, Aristotle sees democracy as grounded on military virtues, and the better democracies are restrained by necessities of production. More than this, polities and middle-class regimes require or imitate the manner in which virtue is a mean while not being directed to virtue as such. Qualifications to serve as or choose assembly members, jurors, and officials, as Aristotle develops his argument, restrain while also honoring the democratic or middling claim. There is no single power that is separated or internally clashing, however, as we find in the United States. And although groups of political friends exist, there are no organized political parties. Indeed, "parties" are the regimes' conflicting claims to rule based on the elements of wealth, freedom, and, to a degree, virtue. This conflict, as we will see, is a ground of revolution.

Our liberal democracies differ from Aristotle in these political ways, and more. The economic expansion I mentioned is an outlet, through economic enterprise, for human spiritedness, or imperial ambition, in a manner that reduces political clash because the opportunities for rule are less limited. And, under proper circumstances, this spiritedness leads to economic growth. This is not so in Aristotle, where virtue finds its home politically or intellectually. Moreover, the liberal virtues that I mentioned are not virtues in Aristotle, although we may think of the fullest responsibility as approaching, or being a democratic version of, greatness of soul. We defend religious toleration that, as I said, over time becomes for many religious indifference and an attack on religion. But religious toleration is not a virtue in Aristotle. Industriousness is a virtue for us, not, as for him, a slavish quality. We prize a general civility—to all—rather than different relationships to ruler and ruled and among the ruled, and different friendships. Our government is meant to represent interests, not form a way of life.

How, then, does Aristotle set the ground for understanding liberal democracy? First, he makes clear that the heart of politics is the regime and that regimes favor ways of life, a perception easy to lose in liberal democracy, given our social, economic, educational, and religious freedom and the view that government is limited to representing interests. Connected to this understanding of regimes is the importance of character, virtue, civic education, and like-mindedness among citizens. For liberal democracy to be successful and for citizens in liberal democracy to be successful, a certain character is necessary. Notions that our liberal democratic regime can succeed simply though a mechanical balancing of institutions or through unchecked economic activity are wrong. Responsibility, industriousness, civility, and toleration are necessary, as are liberal democratic versions of Aristotle's basic virtues, because character and devotion to a just regime do not exist automatically. Developing good character and early civic education are necessary. So too is prudent judgment. Indeed, Aristotle enables us to grasp much of what is best in any democracy or polity:

self-rule, honor, pride, and various virtues. Our excessive legalism and bureaucracy usurp some of the territory of prudence, but prudence remains as vital as ever in order to understand our goals, the proper approach to them, and the balance among them. It is on these grounds, indeed, that bureaucracy can be controlled.

Moreover, although our country's size and scope obviously differ from Aristotle's cities, his understanding of the purpose and requirements of just government indicate much of what one seeks to recapture in our new world, something true of his discussion of family and friendship as well. We attempt to imitate some of city's virtues through federalism and voluntary associations while trying to keep the natural divisions of politics at bay through separation of powers and legitimate political parties.

One should not give up the universal human height made clear in equal natural rights—the divinity to be revered in each of us—or the human spiritedness expressed in private enterprise and many of the goods it produces. Yet what remains necessary at root for human happiness or excellence, individually and in common, is clarified in Aristotle. This is especially necessary when our technology threatens to overcome humanity itself. There is no political perfection that is possible for reasons Aristotle suggests, but liberal democracy can be elevated and stabilized by imitating in our own circumstances the virtues he outlines and the prudence and practices of just political orders.

Discussion: Freedom

It is therefore also appropriate to examine the meaning and importance of freedom to the degree that the *Ethics* and *Politics* clarifies this, for freedom here is the ground on which later views rest and from which they not always correctly depart.

Aristotle's understanding of freedom involves five phenomena. First are the free democrats who contribute to the city's defense—freedom as not being controlled or directed by others and as demanding the honor of rule. Second is the understanding of freedom by extreme democrats as doing whatever one desires. Third is the connection of freedom and rule to spiritedness, mentioned above, to which Aristotle points in his discussion of the best regime. Fourth is freedom as virtue, as freedom simply in the sense of directing oneself to measured enjoyment.[4] The lover of virtue who acts nobly is the one who is free. The step from what is bestial in us, yet humanized through virtue and prudence, begins most clearly with liberality and reaches its peak in complete ethical virtue, not to mention intellectual virtue. Why? To be free is to guide oneself through reason, which measures and authoritatively directs choice once we have a character that sees and looks to see in certain ways. To be free is to be self-directing and, to the degree possible, unimpeded.

This suggests the fifth phenomenon central to freedom in Aristotle's view, namely, freedom as choice, and this primarily means freedom as beginning, as being the first or the principle. Freedom is to begin but to begin properly by choosing properly according to the "end" seen not as a stopping point but as complete activity, or the direction consonant with complete activity. In this sense, what is good simply and pleasant simply is connected to freedom simply, not to freedom as doing whatever one desires. Such freedom is not possible without political freedom—hence, not to be dominated politically and legally or to be enslaved. To be free is to begin, to be the source of one's actions, in choice and, ultimately, virtuous choice, without which (and lacking self-restraint) one is inhibited in one's actions. Philosophical freedom, beyond ethical freedom, is self-direction to the true beginnings.

This understanding of freedom is the ground from which our view of freedom is a narrowing because our view rests on satisfying desire and directing oneself to this, when desires are commensurable and equally worthy to fulfill within the limits of the laws that secure equal rights. An orientation to what is noble, to what is beautiful and choiceworthy in itself, is possible but difficult in liberalism. Our freedom contracts from its simple and natural base, although it widens the number of people who enjoy it. This widening is naturally grounded on, even if does not always recognize, the spiritedness and reverence that reject slavery and the virtues and the heights of which we are capable. Equal natural rights are truly founded on equal honor but need Aristotelian help or even guidance to be used and defended properly, privately and publicly. We require advanced technology for defense and to meet expanded necessity, but it too needs guidance from an understanding of human virtue. And citizens in a country of our great size and bureaucratic complexity need to consider what this complexity harms or neglects and guide bureaucratic action through prudent understanding of our ends, advance like-mindedness among citizens, and permit generous outlets for human spiritedness.[5]

Revolution

What Aristotle now needs to discuss (in Book V) are the sources from which changes in regimes occur. All speak about justice and proportional equality but go astray about it, believing that because they are all alike as free they are equal simply or because they are unequal in wealth (or family) they are wholly unequal. Their claims have a certain justice but not justice simply, and when they do not participate in government there is factional conflict. Those who could most be factional but are least factional "are those who are outstanding in virtue." Some factionalism is directed at changing the regime, others to controlling, loosening, or tightening it. All agree that justice simply is based on merit, that is, equality based on a ratio rather than number or size, but disagree, in the ways mentioned, about equal and unequal merit. One must use numerical equality in some matters and proportional equality and merit in others. Oligarchy and democracy are the most prevalent regimes, for few have high birth and virtue—not more than one hundred.[6] Democracy is more stable than oligarchy, however, because oligarchies have factions against themselves and the people but democracies, only against oligarchy. The regime drawn from the middle is the most stable.

Aristotle (chapter 2) turns to the general causes of factional conflict and revolution: the condition of men who engage in it, that for the sake of which they do it, and its beginning points. They aim at equality or preeminence, engage over profit or honor, and are provoked in several ways. "Dissimilarity of stock is also conducive to faction until they draw breath together" (*Politics* 1303a25–26). Still another occasion is when one part of the city grows in size, for example, when Athenian naval power at Salamis strengthened democracy.

Aristotle then discusses these matters at length, with many examples. Although these issues are large, moreover, the occasions may be small, such as an erotic conflict among the powerful. "One should be wary when such things are beginning in order to head off faction among the powerful" (*Politics* 1303b27–28).

These are universal causes of revolution, but one can also divide by regimes. Democracies most often change because of demagogues' wanton behavior, inciting the multitude or unjustly accusing the rich, who unite against them. Oligarchies change by treating the multitude unjustly or when oligarchs become rivals and "seek popularity" with the many. An oligarchy that is like-minded is not easily changed from within.

Change in oligarchies (and polities) can also arise incidentally, for example, through the spread of the ability to meet property qualifications. In aristocracies, factions arise "when there is some multitude . . . who presume they are similar on the basis of virtue" (*Politics* 1306b28–29). Most often polities and aristocracies are brought down "by a deviation from justice in the regime itself," for example, if democracy and oligarchy "are not beautifully mixed in polity" (*Politics* 1307a7–9). In general, aristocracy is prone to change to oligarchy (and all aristocracies "have an oligarchic character") and polity, to democracy. Especially in aristocracies, change can be imperceptible because whenever a small thing is given up with regard to the regime it becomes easier to give up large things "until they change the entire order" (*Politics* 1307b6). Regimes are also sometimes undone from the outside, moreover, as the Athenians overthrew oligarchies everywhere and the Spartans overthrew democracies.

Aristotle now turns to the preservation of regimes both in common and separately for each. To grasp what destroys them is to grasp what preserves them. For "opposites produce opposites." One safeguard, he again suggests, is to guard against departure from the laws, especially in small matters "since the whole and all things are not something small but composed from the small" (*Politics* 1307b37–38). Other safeguards are not to trick the multitude, not to act unjustly, to (in oligarchies) treat each other properly, to promote fear that the regime might be overturned, to watch for faction, to tighten or loosen property qualifications, to bestow small honors over a long time rather than great ones over a small time, to keep things in harmonious proportion, to oversee those who live (privately) in a way detrimental to their regime, to mix the many needy and the well-off or increase the middle group, and, "a very great thing," to arrange it so that one cannot profit from offices. Having offices open to everyone is democratic, and having the prominent be in office is aristocratic; having no profit to be made from offices brings this about. Moreover, in democracies the property and income of the wealthy ought not to be redistributed, and the rich should be prevented from taking on useless public benefactions such as sponsoring choruses and running torch races.[7] In oligarchies, "much care should be taken of the poor," giving them those offices that have incomes and controlling arrogance and limiting inheritances. In democracies and oligarchies those classes with a lesser share in government should have equality except in the regime's authoritative offices.

Aristotle begins chapter 9 by stating that "those who are going to rule in authoritative offices" should "love the established regime," have "a great capacity for the work involved in rule," and have "the virtue and justice that is relative to that regime." ("For, if justice is not the same in all regimes, justice must necessarily be different.")[8] If these qualities do not exist in one person, look, for the relevant office, for the less widely shared trait (e.g., experience in generals). One needs virtue or at least self-restraint, however, even if one has the other two. The principle of "great importance" is that the multitude that wants the regime is "superior to those not wanting it" (*Politics* 1309b16–17). But "the greatest" of the things mentioned to make regimes last, "now slighted by all," is "education" (and habituation) "relative to the regime" (*Politics* 1310a12–15). This means what allows the regime to be run oligarchically or democratically. Two things seem to define democracy, the majority having authority and freedom. "Justice is held to be something equal," and then (erroneously) whatever seems equal to the majority is authoritative, while doing whatever one wants is freedom. "To live with a view toward the regime," however, "should not be supposed to be slavery, but preservation" (*Politics* 1310a35–36).

In chapter 10 and what follows Aristotle turns to what preserves and destroys monarchy and tyranny. Kingship corresponds to aristocracy based on personal or family virtue, high birth, or beneficent acts, and "tyranny is composed of the ultimate sort of oligarchy and democracy"—a harmful combination of two bad things with its goals of wealth, mistrust of the multitude, and covert and overt destruction of the notables. "The tyrant's goal is pleasure, the goal of a king is the beautiful" (*Politics* 1311a4–5).

Monarchies are changed through sources "pretty much" the same as in other regimes: injustice, especially arrogance, fear, and contempt. It is those reckless by nature (and with military honor) who attack tyrants from contempt for them, "for courage holding power is recklessness" (*Politics* 1312a20). Still others attack monarchs to gain reputation from others.

Tyrannies are destroyed from the outside or from within, also from contempt—often for the lives of gratification of tyrants' successors—hatred, and anger. Anger is a consequence of the spiritedness aroused by arrogance and has less room for reasoning than does hatred. Extreme oligarchies and democracies are "tyrannies divided." Kingship is destroyed from within by factions or when kings become more tyrannical; it no longer arises today because too many are alike to submit to it voluntarily.

Kingship and tyranny are preserved by the opposite causes of what has been mentioned, kingship, in particular, by becoming more moderate and reducing matters over which kings have authority. Tyrannies are preserved by doing things such as "lopping off the preeminent and eliminating those with high thoughts, and, also, not permitting common messes, clubs [and] education," using spies, forcing activity to be in the open, stirring up slander, impoverishing subjects, being a warmonger, and otherwise limiting leisure, advancing female control of the house and permissiveness to slaves (as in democracies' last stages), and encouraging flatterers (*Politics* 1313a40–1313b1). Tyranny, in short, aims to make its subjects small souled, distrustful, and incapable.

The almost opposite way to preserve tyranny is to make it more kingly, as long as the tyrant safeguards his power so that he can rule the unwilling as well as the willing. While this remains his purpose, he should "give a beautiful performance of the part of the kingly ruler," being held to be thoughtful about common funds; appearing dignified, not harsh, so others feel awe, not fear, in encountering him; cultivating a military reputation; not acting arrogantly; being moderate in pleasures; acting as a steward; "showing himself to be seriously attentive to the things related to the gods" (without silliness); honoring citizens; having punishments meted out by others; and letting no one be great or if any, several (*Politics* 1314b39–40). Aristotle also remarks the difference between honor and wealth as motives against a tyrant: it is spirited anger against humiliating arrogance that will pay the price of its life. A tyrant should also keep both of the city's parts (rich and poor) safe and use the stronger one as part of his rule. In short, he should appear managerial, kingly, and a steward and pursue moderation. By following these measures, he will be virtuous or, at least, half decent and half vicious. One could make one's tyranny last longer this way, but, in any event, tyrannies (and oligarchies) are short lived. Aristotle then concludes his discussion by criticizing Socrates's discussion of revolution in the *Republic*. He again avoids mentioning the *Republic*'s rule of philosophers while subtly recognizing the movement from Socrates's tyrannical regime to the best one.

Discussion: Revolution

Aristotle's discussion here adds to our understanding of the practices and activities of regimes. One might argue, however, that Aristotle's view of revolution is cogent but limited. It does not explain well the American, French, or Russian Revolution, the Chinese Revolution, or the dominance of Nazi tyranny. It falls short especially in seeing the appeal to the many and the universalism or ethnic superiority displayed, or claimed to be displayed, in some of these revolutions. Yet if one strips away fancy justifications for rule Aristotle's discussion of tyranny, oligarchy (especially if the ruling few are not merely the propertied, although they soon become this), and democracy is perhaps sufficient or nearly sufficient to understand and judge revolution. Beginning from this understanding and not departing from it too quickly allows one to judge revolutions in terms of their degree of natural justice. This is also true of the international aspects of revolution, for as Aristotle reminds us, Athens and Sparta each overthrew cities governed by the other's regime.

One might say, nonetheless, that the attempted universality or ethnic breadth of many modern revolutions' rhetorical appeal also limits the utility of Aristotle's analysis. Can we understand the methods of propaganda and enlightenment—as distinguished from their desirability—in Aristotle's terms? Is there something new in the way that conviction is established? Or does his discussion in the *Rhetoric* (and the *Poetics*) exhaust or sufficiently address how to control the passions and moods of mass audiences and achieve desired effects from them? One would be hard pressed to say what is new in the understanding of effects—as differentiated from the novelty of some methods.[9] The central question concerns the originality of the universality of religion and religious appeal and its revolutionary understanding of happiness, or the human end. Here we might suggest that the heart of the appeal is to equality, religiously, but often with inequality in hierarchy and with the power of fear (of the afterlife) being central politically.

Aristotle's (and Plato's) understanding of the dominance of opinions about "just" equality and inequality is still the crucial first (and large) step in understanding the attraction of claims to political/religious universality or claims to ethnic mastery, and his view of virtue is the crucial step in judging their worth. The relatively greater later independence of imperial religion from political control can create novel problems of governance. But it does not lead to a properly novel understanding of regimes. Nor does it change the natural standpoint from which to assess religious claims.[10]

A related problem occurs once philosophy loses its independence because some regimes claim to be based on "scientific" truth, beyond even the utility and, hence, subordination, of modern science. The danger here is how political claims to rest on undoubtable truth restrict openness of inquiry and attention to perplexity. The danger arises as well from the need to enforce political uniformity against the natural and never altogether justly resolvable disputes that stem from honor, freedom, and virtue. The danger to philosophy is true also from religions that claim to subsume philosophical truth. We might say, however, that these issues are considered with special depth in Aristotle's and Plato's discussion of the superiority, yet limits, of intellectual virtue. On the whole, Aristotle's understanding of the justice, happiness, and variety of regimes is indispensable for recognizing and judging the worth and causes of revolutions.[11]

Aristotle surfaces large and small natural causes of change in regimes. The different claims to rule that define different regimes mean that every regime is unstable or that its perpetuation needs to be managed carefully. The possibilities for change in regimes are limited, but the occasions for change are many. These occasions themselves belong to necessity and, especially, to the nature of arrogance, anger, and offended pride. The growth of a middle class, the range from poor to rich, the movement in economic status, and, especially, the control and redirection of pride and honor—not its restriction altogether but the expansion of private and public outlets for it—encourage relative stability in modern liberal democracies. Nonetheless, civic education—education in what justifies our regime's way of life—remains a necessary condition of this stability. Aristotle provides a template for preserving decent ways of life and an understanding of the practices of tyranny that we must counter.

Chapter Seven

Political Excellence and Its Limits

Political Restrictions and the Confines of Virtue: Offices and Democracies

In Book VI of the *Politics* Aristotle more fully discusses the various forms of democracy and other regimes and the several ways to combine oligarchic, aristocratic, and democratic procedures in deliberation, judging, and offices. Democracies vary by the different types of multitudes who predominate in them, farmers, workers, and laborers, and in the way that they combine procedures. "It is useful to be familiar with these things" for instituting and reforming democracies. Democracies' premise is freedom. Democrats think freedom is ruling and being ruled in turn but equally based on number, not merit, so that what the majority resolves is justice. Indeed, they also think freedom is living as one wants—not to be ruled at all or in turn. This starting point leads to things such as choosing almost all offices from all, by lot, with little or no property qualification, with short duration in office, where all judge, where the assembly is the final authority, where there is payment, and where lack of family background, vulgarity, and poverty are thought suited for popular rule. But, Aristotle suggests, the most just democratic equality would be for everyone—not only the poor—to have equal authority in a way that balances numbers and assessments.

The democracy devoted to farming is best, for farmers' time is occupied in dealing with necessities, not politics, and they generally prefer work, "for the many strive more for profit than for honor" (*Politics* 1318b16-17). Their wish for honor is satisfied by having authority over electing and reviewing officials and being jurors, with higher offices held according to some property qualification or by the decent. (A way to advantage farming is by controlling landownership.) The next best population for democracy is found among herders; they are similar to farmers. The other sorts are inferior and debased, doing no work of virtue, and being too easily available for assemblies.

Aristotle then reminds us that the legislators and laws need to consider what helps the regime be preserved, not what makes it more democratic (or oligarchic), for example, not confiscating property and giving it to the people, penalizing frivolous lawsuits, and not handing out surplus revenue, which becomes a "punctured jar." For "instituting it is not the greatest or only task of the legislator or those wishing to constitute a [democratic] regime, but, rather, to see that it is preserved; for it is not difficult to be governed in one fashion or another for one, two, or three days" (*Politics* 1319b34-37). The many should not be overly poor: surpluses should be distributed to allow them to "start in a trade or farming." In oligarchies (whose best blended sort is close to polity) one should divide property qualifications into lower and higher amounts, corresponding to participation in merely necessary or more authoritative offices. Whoever meets the property qualification should be allowed to take part in government.

In chapter 7 Aristotle turns to the connection between arms and regimes. When one can have large estates and horses, it is "natural to build up a strong oligarchy," where inhabitants' safety is secured by the power of cavalry. The next sort of oligarchy is natural where the land is suited for heavy arms. "But the light-armed and naval powers are entirely suited to popular rule." Skilled generals join the three forces. Oligarchs need to be taught light-armed and unarmed tactics because without knowing these democrats will prevail over them, as light arms can defeat heavy arms and cavalry. Oligarchies should make room for the people in administration, but the most authoritative offices should have obligations such as magnificent sacrifices and public monuments so that the people are both willing not to have these offices and to see the government stay in power.

Aristotle next turns to dividing offices "in a beautiful way," including, first, offices for necessary affairs such as markets, property, roads, revenues, and punishments of convicts and debtors. These latter offices are difficult to fill because they incur hostility. It is impossible for men to be partners, however, if one cannot have lawsuits and if punishments cannot be carried out.[1] Those who judge and punish and those who guard prisoners should be split, and the same punishers should not be in office continuously.

Aristotle then discusses necessary offices with a higher rank that require experience and trust, such as generalships and auditors, and the office, such as that of preliminary councilors or law guardians, "that is most particularly authoritative over all matters," having "final dispositions as well as the introduction of all measures, or presiding over the multitude wherever the people have authority" (*Politics* 1322b12-15). There are also priests and officials who deal with sacred matters whose offices are not clearly "political" but are "necessary sorts of superintendence" and, for cities with more leisure and mindful of good order, overseers of women and children and supervisors of athletic and dramatic competitions. In democracies the poor lack slaves and need to use women and children as attendants.[2]

Self-Restraint

I return now to the *Ethics*, namely, Aristotle's discussion in Book VII of self-restraint and its lack. For this makes clear the possibility of proper choice and action even in the absence of sufficient excellence and is in this sense similar to his discussion of regimes that approach virtue, although they fall short of it.

Aristotle presents Book VII as "another beginning" to his *Ethics*. It follows his reminder in his discussion of prudence that pleasure can distort virtuous principles but not mathematical ones.[3] Self-restraint describes the limits of those who are ordinarily respectable but lack the rigor of unrelenting virtuous choice and action.

Vice, lack of self-restraint, and brutishness should be avoided, he begins: vice's contrary is virtue, lack of self-restraint's contrary is self-restraint, and brutishness's contrary is the divine. Gods' character, however, is not an excess of virtue. Rather, it is more honorable than virtue. And (human) brutes are rare. Aristotle thus now discusses self-restraint and its lack and steadfastness as opposed to softness and delicacy. Chapter 2 lays out various perplexities concerning self-restraint, beginning with Socrates's view that opposes "the phenomena that come plainly to sight." For Socrates claimed that self-restraint cannot be lacking in one who knows: he argued that nobody acts contrary to what is best while supposing he so acts. In chapter 3 Aristotle makes his central point: lack of self-restraint simply involves things that concern the licentious, but someone licentious believes that he ought always to pursue pleasure, while someone who lacks self-restraint does not think this but pursues pleasure anyway. Lacking self-restraint can occur together with knowledge or strong opinion: having but not exercising knowledge of the universal or of the minor premise. However, actively knowing both and still lacking restraint would cause wonder. Someone gripped by spiritedness or sexual desire may have but not use his knowledge. Moreover, two reasonable universals may conflict with an unreasonable one, advanced by desire. Animals, by contrast, "do not lack self-restraint" "because they do not possess a universal conviction but, rather, an image and memory of particulars" (*Ethics* 1147b4-6). Indeed, it is the final point, the knowledge bound up with perception, that is overcome in lack of self-restraint, not knowledge itself, and to this extent Socrates is correct. Lack of self-restraint simply concerns bodily pleasures, not being unrestrained with regard to honor, victory, or other pleasant things: unrestrained spiritedness is lacking in self-restraint only by analogy or similarity or metaphorically. Indeed, lack of self-restraint from spiritedness is "less shameful" than that from desire. Spiritedness's "heated and swift nature" harms reason but only partially. And it is often more natural than excessive desire.

Some things are pleasant by nature, and of these some are pleasant simply and others only with regard to various kinds of animals and humans. Still other pleasures arise through people's defective habits or corrupt natures. Hence, there is corruption of humans simply or corruption in relation to one of these.

The licentious person lacks restraint by choice, not by being defeated, as is the case with someone who (occasionally) lacks self-restraint. While self-restraint overpowers having a strong desire (for example), steadfastness holds out against it. It does not give in. Softness in what most can hold out against (e.g., excessive amusement) can be natural, for example, with women as opposed to men. Some impetuously do not abide by deliberations, while others are led by passion because they do not deliberate. The licentious, moreover, do not feel regret, as those who lack self-restraint do, so the latter are curable but not the former. It is virtue that preserves the proper principle on which one acts.[4]

Starting with chapter 11 we receive Aristotle's first long analysis of pleasure, which I already discussed. For pleasure is what lack of self-restraint primarily concerns.

Aristotle's recognition of our imperfections, without ire or excuse, is visible as well in his discussions of shame and in his political analysis, with its discussion of the variety of deficient regimes. Shame, he tells us in the *Rhetoric*, is "a certain pain and perturbation pertaining to those bad things (present, past, and future) that appear to bring disrepute," and shamelessness is a slighting of or "apathetic indifference" to these.[5] "The many are not naturally obedient to the governance supplied by a sense of shame," he remarks in the *Ethics*, "but rather to that supplied by fear" (*Ethics* 1179b10). Someone virtuous should not perform shameful acts, but it is better to feel shame than to be shameless, and shame is perhaps especially important in teaching good habits to the young.

Discussion: Democracy

The limits of politics are rooted in the impossibility of a perfect solution to the problem of the different justified claims to rule. These limits are the ground of Aristotle's political caution or, if one likes, his conservatism—his understanding of the restrictions in implementing excellence and perfection without fostering indifference, defeatism, or cynicism. Aristotle's understanding here, and his political cleverness or prudence, is especially visible in his discussion of democracy, because he believes that democracy is the future's likeliest regime. His discussion points out phenomena that are important for the justice and stability of any democracy, subtle ways to recognize but also limit the rule of the people or "direct" democracy: an attempt to favor politically those among the people with the least inclination to govern, for example, farmers, or those whose own advantage will lead them to be least unjust; a reminder that a majority might be composed of some of the rich together with some of the poor; and a concern to balance quantity with quality. It is or should be possible for prudent legislators or founders, such as our own, to see the salience of these points and directives, whatever the differences among institutional options.

Discussion: The Harshness of Politics

Aristotle discusses politics primarily in terms of the justice of regimes, their link to happiness, and the meeting of necessities. But he does not overlook, indeed he subtly features, the harshness or danger of political life. He downplays this rhetorically, however, or makes few if any statements about this harshness as such. Indeed, one can see in his discussion of punishment the degree to which the need for this harshness is covered over by citizens, at least among themselves. It is visible in Aristotle, however, even if softened rhetorically. It is a vital part of Aristotle's discussion, and the elements he addresses remain fundamental: the basic harshness of political life can never be ignored. Will one's neighbors leave one alone? Not always. Losing in war can mean full loss of political freedom; at the least it means limits on resources and territory. And to lose a war is not only to risk losing free rule. It is also to risk being enslaved. Political communities must therefore attend to war, to defense, and, if necessary, to what they require to expand. The Spartan helots (indeed, any slaves who attempt to revolt) do not appear to be the extreme version of Aristotle's natural slaves, and they are not obviously ruled by those with full deliberative reason. Yet they are treated effectively as slaves.

Aristotle's discussion of the significance of light and heavy arms and cavalry, as well as his discussion of common messes, goes beyond defending oneself against others. It points also to the connection between force and rule within cities themselves.

The existence of slavery and the importance of being ready for war are not the only areas in which Aristotle points to the harshness of political life. He mentions ostracism frequently. A legislator should arrange matters so that ostracism is unnecessary, but it occurs in practice—and, presumably, not only because the one ostracized is too impressive to be treated equally. One reason that judicial rhetoric is so important is because of the number of false accusations faced by prominent or wealthy citizens. Moreover, groups of citizens are forced or permitted to colonize. Are these colonies sent only to unoccupied territory or also to already occupied territory (even if minimally)? We meet necessities economically through farming and commerce, but the need first to take one's own land is clear on reflection if not emphasized.

Aristotle's most extensive examination of not only the harshness but also the fragility of political life is in his discussion of revolution. Each regime can become another because each of the three elements that deserve a share in rule almost always believes that its share is insufficient in practice. And within regimes based on freedom, wealth and (perhaps) virtue seen as good birth are each prone to believe that the actual rulers or ruling group is insufficiently worthy. Moreover, there are reasons, primarily arrogance or pride, that lead some to seek to overthrow rulers. Political stability is thus always in question. Whatever the justice of a regime, it will not last unless the strongest elements in the city wish it to remain. Just communities are fragile and political life difficult. Aristotle makes this fragility clear.

The Best Regime

In Books VII and VIII of the *Politics* Aristotle turns to discussing the best regime. Given what we have explored, much of what he says is unsurprising, but there are discussions that add to what we have seen.

"Concerning the best regime," he begins, "anyone who is going to investigate it appropriately must necessarily discuss first the most choiceworthy way of life" (*Politics* 1323a15–17). We are happy in relation to virtue and good judgment and actions in accord with these.[6] The best city is happy, and its beautiful deeds (and citizens) are impossible without virtue. The "courage, justice, and prudence, of a city have the same power and shape" as the just and prudent things in which individuals share (*Politics* 1323b34–35).

All agree that a happy city is what they believe a happy individual to be (e.g., wealthy). Would one be happier, however, if free from the political community? Is a political and active life preferable or, rather, one divorced from external things (e.g., a life of contemplation), "which some assert is the only philosophic way of life" (*Politics* 1324a29). These are the choices for those "most ambitious with a view toward virtue." Some think ruling other cities as a master is unjust or a hindrance to one's well-being; others, that greater virtue occurs in those who act in common, or master cities. But how could dominating others, which can be done unjustly, belong to statesmanship? Force does not belong in the other arts, and we seek just rule among ourselves. One should seek to master only those naturally meant to be mastered, not those naturally free. An isolated city would be happy on its own while not being organized for war: warlike pursuits are regarded as noble but are not the highest end.

The life of someone free is better than one that involves mastery. Not every rule is mastery, however. Is it best to have authority over everyone? "Among similar persons what is beautiful and just consists in taking turns." Inequality for equals and unlikeness for those who are alike is contrary to nature, "and nothing contrary to nature is beautiful" (*Politics* 1325b7–10).

Indeed, "thoughts that are complete in themselves" and "contemplations and thoughts that are for their own sake" are more active than actions directed to others, and for consequences. For "their end is acting well, so that too is action," and even in external actions master craftsmen (whose activity is thinking) act most authoritatively (*Politics* 1325b20–24). Moreover, the parts of cities interact (and, therefore, their actions need not be warlike) as do human beings. Indeed, the god and the whole cosmos have no external actions beyond what is proper to themselves—and one would not say that they are not in beautiful condition. So, Aristotle concludes, "the same way of life must necessarily be best both for each human being individually and for cities and human beings in common" (*Politics* 1325b31–33).[7]

Aristotle turns next to the underlying (but not impossible) conditions—the equipment—for the best city. The statesman and legislator, as other artisans, need suitable material. First is population. A city that is too populous will not have good laws; rather, one needs a number capable of forming a beautiful order. This is "a work requiring divine power, which is what holds together the totality" (*Politics* 1326a32–33). Each thing has the power that belongs to it, which cannot exist if it is either too large or small. Cities if too small are not self-sufficient and if too large (as a nation is) cannot have a regime or live well. "The best limit for a city is this: the greatest excess of number surpassing self-sufficiency of life that is easily surveyable" (*Politics* 1326b23–24).

Territory concerns "something similar." Everyone praises what is self-sufficient and allows citizens' leisure, combining freedom and moderation. One wants easy exit and conveyance of goods and things, difficulty of penetration, what is easy to survey (and, therefore, to defend), and what is well situated with regard to land and sea.

What should the nature of the people be? To stay free and well governed and to be guided to virtue by a legislator, a people needs to be both thoughtful and spirited. Spiritedness produces friendliness "since it is the power in the soul by which we feel friendship."[8] Ruling and freedom "stem from this for everyone because spiritedness is expert in ruling and indomitable" (*Politics* 1328a6–7). But (contra Plato) "the spirited are not harsh toward the unknown": the great souled are not savage by nature but only toward the unjust, especially intimates who have harmed them.

Not everything the city needs is a part of it—in what is according to nature things without which a whole could not exist are not parts of it. Possessions in a city, including animate things, are distinguished from the community of those who are similar for the sake of practicing virtue. Different cities and regimes arise from differences in sharing this. Cities need, as parts, tasks related to food, arts, arms, funds, fifth (and first) priestcraft, and, most necessary of all, judgment about the advantageous and just. Cities need these to be self-sufficient and are organized to exercise these functions.

In a city with men who are just simply, the citizens ought not to come from or share in every part—for example, not farmers or artisans (or traders). For citizens need leisure. Those who deliberate about advantage and justice do share military functions, for those with power cannot always be ruled, and they control whether government endures. The priesthood should go to the deliberating (but not the arms-bearing) part: it is fitting for those who are weary to serve the gods and have rest for themselves.

Indeed, "it seems to be something familiar to those philosophizing about the regime not only at present or in recent times" that the city should be divided among separate types of people (*Politics* 1329b1–3). Practically everything has "been discovered on many"—or infinite—occasions "in the course of time": for need teaches necessities and then what is related to elegance and superfluity. So too with regimes. We should adopt what has been satisfactory and seek what has been left out. Possessions should be used commonly, as among friends, but not held in common. There should be common as well as private land, and private land should be divided between city and frontiers (to give all a stake in both). Farmers themselves should be slaves, not of one stock if spirited, or unspirited barbarians; freedom may in some way be held out as a reward for slaves.

Common meals should be provided in guardhouses and, for the highest officials, in "buildings assigned to divine matters." There should be common meals for priests, and temples are to be distributed throughout, some for gods and some for heroes. It is pointless to give more precise details, Aristotle concludes, for what is difficult in these matters is not understanding but doing. Speaking about them is a "work of prayer, having them come about, of chance" (*Politics* 1331b20–23).

Discussing the regime comes next. Living well comes from rightly positing the end of actions and discovering the actions related to the end, and we can be wrong in either or both regards. Happiness is the activity and complete practice of virtue, not on the basis of a premise but simply, that is, beautifully. Just actions such as punishment stem from virtue but are matters of necessity. It is more choiceworthy not to need them. Someone with virtue finds the good things simply to be good. We pray for the city to obtain that over which chance has authority, but the city's excellence is the work of knowledge and choice. The key question is how all the citizens may be excellent, for a city is excellent through all its citizens' excellence.

All citizens must share in ruling and being ruled in turn, because none has such superiority in body and soul that this superiority is obvious and beyond dispute. (We see, therefore, that the best city is not one ruled by someone with virtue that surpasses all others in it.) Nature distinguishes between the old and the young, and the young will not chafe at being ruled, especially because they will have their turn. So rulers and ruled are the same and different, as is their education.

The soul has two parts, what has reason and what can obey it. The worse, in art and nature, is for the better, here the part with reason. Reason is divided into practical and theoretical and the virtues belonging to them. The most choiceworthy for a person is the highest he can attain (i.e., theoretical or practical reason and actions).[9] Life is also split, between business and leisure, war and peace, necessary and beautiful actions. As with the choice of actions of the parts of the soul, war must be for peace, business for leisure, necessary and useful actions for the sake of the beautiful. The political rulers' laws should give priority to ends, to what is better. And children should be educated in these aims.

"The same things are best for men both privately and in common, and the legislator should implant these in the souls of human beings" (*Politics* 1333b35–38). One should train in war in order not to be enslaved, to lead for the benefit of the ruled, and to master those who deserve to be slaves. But one should educate primarily for living at leisure. Some of the virtues one aims at are for leisure and pastimes and some to deal with necessities in order to have leisure and not be enslaved by attackers. Hence, one, and the city, needs courage and endurance for occupations, moderation for leisure, and justice at both times and even more in leisure. One especially needs philosophy, moderation, and justice amid "an abundance of good things."

Nature, habit, and reason should be harmonious. Habits (and birth) should be for reason and intellect, nature's end. Desire and spiritedness in the soul are for the sake of the intellect, and the body is for the sake of the soul. The legislator thus first needs to see that the bodies of children are best. Aristotle then discusses the best times for marriage and exercise and other matters appropriate for young children. Adultery (relations with another man or woman) is to be punished as not beautiful.

Aristotle turns next to education and to music (in the literal sense), as discussed above. In rhythms and melodies, he proceeds to argue, likenesses exist of the nature of anger and gentleness and also "of courage and moderation" and their opposites "and the other states of character" (*Politics* 1340a21–22). We are altered in soul when we listen to these things, and habituation to feel pain and delight in likenesses comes close to a relation to the truth. If one delights in contemplating something's image merely for the form, it necessarily follows that contemplating the thing itself will be pleasing. Likenesses to states of character are not present to the other sense perceptions, except to a degree in sight (of statues), but as indications, not imitations. In tunes, however, there are "images of states of character." Different modes of music obviously put one in different states; one does not have the same experience with each—softer, moderate, and inspired. This is also true of rhythmic motions. "This is what those who have philosophized in connection with this sort of education, have argued, and nobly: they find proofs for their arguments in the deeds themselves" (*Politics* 1340b5–7).

It is difficult seriously to judge activities in which one has not taken part. Children need to be kept occupied: "education is a rattle for the young when they are bigger." Children should therefore take part in musical activities so that when older they are competent to judge what is beautiful and enjoy it correctly. This does not make them artisans, for one can consider the sorts of melodies, rhythms, and instruments to the proper, not professional, extent, with the true good being what contributes to political virtue.[10]

Aristotle then discusses harmonies and rhythm, in outline, "in legal fashion," with details found by looking to experts in music and those in philosophy who are also experienced in music education. As those engaged in philosophy distinguish them, the modes are adopted to character, action, or inspiration, with "the nature of harmonies" akin to each one. For education, tunes and harmonies that depict character (e.g., the Dorian mode) should be used, but any one is acceptable if approved by those who are engaged in philosophy and are experienced in music. Aristotle then concludes here by criticizing Socrates in the *Republic*.

I discussed previously Aristotle's understanding of the connection between virtue and politics and questions of war, size, population, and slavery. I discuss below Aristotle's remarks about philosophy and what we learn here about the soul.

Part Three

Speech

Chapter Eight

Friendship and the Soul

I turn now to the third part of this study, Aristotle's discussion of speech, the distinctive power of human beings. I begin with his discussion of friendship in the *Ethics*, which is a bridge between ethical and political understanding and intellectual virtue and then provide a brief summary of his remarks in the *Ethics*, *Politics*, and *Rhetoric* about the soul. I consider next his understanding of everyday speech in the *Rhetoric* and conclude with his understanding of philosophy in the three works.

Friendship

It might seem that Book X's discussion of pleasure in the *Ethics* would follow Aristotle's discussion of pleasure in Book VII, but instead we have two books on friendship. The discussion of friendship therefore expands Aristotle's examination of human affairs or statesmanship and serves as a bridge to his discussion of philosophy and to my discussion of speech generally.

Friendship is a certain virtue or follows it, Aristotle begins Book VIII. None would choose life without friends: they allow the prosperous to benefit others, help guard prosperity, and help the young and old. "By nature" friendship seems inherent between parents and offspring, in birds and animals too, and among those of like kind. And it seems to hold cities together: legislators aim at like-mindedness or lack of discord; they are serious about it for friends, who do not need justice. Moreover, friendship is noble: We praise those who love friends, it is noble to have many, and good men and (good) friends are supposed to be the same.

These are Aristotle's initial statements about the phenomenon, combining what seems to be and what is said about it. After this he proceeds by considering the object of friendship: Is it the good, pleasant, or useful? The good and the pleasant are lovable as ends, either what is good simply or what appears good for oneself. We speak of friendship where there is reciprocated love and wish for the good. "Friends . . . have goodwill toward each other, [and are] not unnoticed in their wishing for the good things for the other" (*Ethics* 1156a2-5).

Friendship has three forms, related to use, the good, and pleasure. Those who are friendly because of utility and pleasure do not love someone in themselves but for the good they bring them; hence, incidentally, with friendships that are easily dissolved. "Complete friendship," however, is the friendship of those "who are good or alike according to virtue" (*Ethics* 1156b6–7). They wish for good things for their friends' sake, and each is good simply and thus also beneficial and pleasant to each other. Such friendships are rare because such people are few, and such friendship needs time and "habits formed by living together." Friendships based on utility (including alliances among cities) and on pleasure resemble this complete friendship, which "is friendship in the primary and authoritative sense" (*Ethics* 1157a30–31). The good are "friends simply."[1]

Friendship is like a habit, not a passion: we wish good things for others in accord with their habits, and in doing so we love this good (the friend) for itself (and in this way love ourselves). What is good or pleasant simply seems lovable or choiceworthy. Separation does not dissolve friendship but does hamper its activity, for friends pass the time together and hence delight in each other's company, as the young do more than the elderly. Moreover, one cannot love many. Eros is like an excess and "arises naturally in relation to one" (*Ethics* 1158a12–13).

Aristotle then indicates that the friendship he has been discussing involves equality, for the friends wish for or exchange the same things.

This sets the stage for "a different form of friendship," one based on inequality, as father for son, an older for a younger man, husband for wife, and ruler for ruled. In each of these the friendship varies because a different virtue, work, or reason for the friendship is involved. The feelings of friendship should be proportional, with the better owed more. When affection accords with merit, equality "somehow" (i.e., here proportionally) arises. When friends differ too much in virtue and resources they are not and do not deem themselves worthy to be friends, as with humans and gods, inferiors and kings, and those worthy of nothing "with the best and wisest." It is said "nobly" that friends do not wish for such great goods for their friends that they no longer remain as they are—for example, becoming gods, not humans. Indeed, one might not wish all human goods for them "since each wishes the good things for himself most of all" (*Ethics* 1159a10–11).

Aristotle next turns to the questions of loving versus being loved. Being loved "seems close" to being honored. Those who delight in honor from the decent aim to confirm their opinion that they are good. Friendship, however, seems more to love than to be loved, as mothers do with their children. He then explores the relation of justice and friendship: friendship and justice exist in every community and are concerned with the same matters and people. They differ in different communities, however, among brothers, say, or for parents. And it is "natural" for what is just to increase with friendship. "All communities are like parts of the political community," which aims at common advantage for life as a whole. The lesser communities, however, are for the sake of only partial advantage. In a tyranny there is little friendship. And where there is nothing in common between ruler and ruled, as in soul to body, artisan to tool, or master to slave, no friendship or justice exists, although the ruled are benefited. A slave is an "animate tool." But as a human being, not as a slave as such, there is friendship, because "there seems to be something just for every human being in relation to everyone able to share in law and contract" (*Ethics* 1161b7–10).

In the three forms of friendship, where the friends are equal, they "ought to love each other equally, in accord with the relevant equality." In friendships among unequals the superior should receive honor, "the one in need, gain." "Honor is the reward of virtue and benefaction." This is true also in regimes. To provide nothing to the community is to not be honored, and "honor is held in common"(*Ethics* 1163b1–8). Sometimes (e.g., with parents) one can never repay what is merited.

The order of Book IX is hardly clear. Its overall topic is wholeness or likeness in friendship and especially the connection between love of self or one's own and what is good. The book begins by indicating that friendship based on character endures and that differences arise when lovers do not receive what they wish. Those who give for their partner's sake have a friendship that accords with virtue, unlike sophists for whom "no one would pay money for what they know," and as with "those who share in philosophy," where honor cannot be balanced and worth is not measured in money. One repays what is possible, as with gods and parents. In general, "repayment is determined with a view to the amount that the recipients' assess." Aristotle then continues the discussion of payment, especially to the incommensurable, and examines the complexities involved in obeying one's father in all, as opposed to obeying artisans, and giving to comrades, as opposed to the virtuous and creditors. Both nobility and necessity matter in considering this, and one should give to each (say, brother or father) the honor due them. Aristotle works through with characteristic common sense the different degrees of honor that we owe to, say, fathers and generals, what we owe to prior and childhood friends, and so on.

In friendship we wish for the life of our friends, and we go through life together with them and share their sufferings and joys, as, for example, with a mother's love. We also see this in the decent person concerning himself: he longs with his whole soul for, and does, good things for himself for his own sake, namely, his thinking part, and he wishes to live, especially his prudent part. One wishes for good things for oneself but not by becoming another (e.g., a god), and the good person goes through life pleasantly, given his memories and hopes. He has objects to contemplate, and his pains and pleasures are the same always. This is also true of one's friend, as another self. The peak of friendship is friendship toward oneself. It seems that there is self-friendship for the virtuous, but the base are divided from or flee from themselves: their souls are formed by faction, and they possess nothing lovable.

Friendship may begin in goodwill for those unaware of one's friendship. Such goodwill is not even friendly feeling, however, for there is no intensity or longing. Love begins with pleasant sight, but delighting in another's looks does not yet mean yearning for the absent person and desiring their presence. Cities are like-minded among their citizens concerning common choices and actions on large matters where they have the same thing in mind in the same way. It is the decent who are (truly) like-minded, wishing for the just and advantageous in common.

Although wanting to be benefited seems more natural or human than being a benefactor, it is benefactors who love more than those benefited, because they love their own, as artisans do their works. The maker lives in the activity and loves his work, that is, himself. This is natural, as is delighting in the object of benefaction, for this is involved in one's noble action. And you love more what you take pains over, as mothers do, who also know more that their children are their own.

Aristotle then considers this perplexity: Should one love oneself most or someone else? The belief that self-love deserves reproach views self-love as taking more money, honor, and pleasure for oneself. The many say this but not about those who secure justice, virtue, and the noble for themselves. But is not the greater self-lover one who takes more of the noblest for the authoritative part in him? The authoritative intellect is oneself: as with other wholes, such as cities, we are most our authoritative part. It is reason that dominates us: deeds with reason are done by oneself and voluntarily, and the good person is a self-lover. Exertion and competition about the noble meet common necessities and bring about the greatest self-good "if virtue is of such a character." The mature man chooses noble things for himself, even giving up honors and offices to a friend and therefore causing his actions.[2]

Happiness once again becomes Aristotle's theme, ostensibly to connect having friends to happiness but also perhaps to indicate that by connecting love of one's own and virtue we are again reaching a peak in ethical virtue, preparing another discussion (in Book X) of the good, pleasure, and intellectual virtue. Do the happy need friends? (Friends are external goods.) Yes, the mature man needs friends in order to do some good: happiness is activity. And we are naturally political. He may not need the usual friends, but he needs other mature ones for acting and to observe their good actions, which is easier than observing his own, and for training. For the decent, what is good by nature (including the pleasant) is good (for him). Living is itself good and pleasant, especially for the good (and decent): in perceiving the good in itself the good feel pleasure and, hence, do so while observing a friend (another or different self). We perceive this good too in living together and sharing in a community of speeches and thoughts. So the blessed have friends.

In the remaining chapters of Book IX Aristotle adds to our understanding of friendship by taking up several issues. More friends than is sufficient for one's life, for pleasure or use, impedes living nobly. For the noble, the measure of quantity is within these limits—the greatest number with whom one could live together nobly. For example, ten is too few and one hundred thousand too many to be a city. Eros is with one and is a peak in excess; intense friendship is (only) with a few. To have too many "friends" is to be obsequious.

Noble friendship, moreover, needs friends more in good fortune than bad. The better or courageous do not want friends to share in misfortune (although seeing friends is pleasant). Still, the presence of friends is choiceworthy in all cases. Indeed, friends want to perceive that the other exists and what this existence is for. They want to be with friends when they engage in the goal for which they choose to live: drink, dice, exercise, hunting, and philosophizing together. The noble improve and are corrected in error by friends.[3]

Discussion: Friendship

As with the other issues I am exploring, Aristotle presents the basic phenomena that later discussions either take for granted or on which they are based. His discussion covers many matters and uses many similar but not identical terms translated as friendship, love, fondness, and affection, among them.[4] The matters he discusses range from commercial friends to philosophical friends and address family, politics, benefactors, and ordinary friends.

We may summarize matters and address ambiguities by considering what Aristotle might mean by calling friendship a virtue but also saying only that it "follows" virtue. If friendship deals with friends in the right way, for the right reason, at the right time and place, it is a virtue, and one's friends would be in accord with virtue. But it also only "follows" virtue because friends for utility or ordinary pleasure fall short of this. Aristotle's discussion is still more complex, however, because he also includes love of family, or love of one's own, in his discussion, as well as political friendship, and he indicates the exclusivity of eros. He discusses these largely but not only in terms of the justice of forms of government—the like-mindedness of citizens and (as discussed above) kingly, aristocratic, and democratic (polity-like) relations in families. In almost all cases we may say that friendship is an attachment to others as an attachment to oneself (and vice versa). In the highest cases this is an attachment to oneself as noble or possibly noble and, hence, to virtue.

This orientation to the noble is true too in the city and the family, which are directed to virtue in the best cases—one's own, one's family's, and one's fellow citizens'. It is also so, however, that attachment to others as oneself requires attention to meeting their necessities as well as one's own necessities. Friendship here is (only) like virtue, just as one's choice of friends is restricted because of friendship for oneself, one's family, and, usually, one's city. One should seek the best or most noble for them, but they, and oneself, will normally have priority over other possibly more excellent friends. One would hardly praise, and either condemn or pity, those who ignore their city or family or act as if they can be sufficient on their own. Friendship toward oneself, in this extended sense, is a condition of excellence. At the same time, if attention to what is most one's own—one's intellect or reason, one's mind—leads toward philosophical activity one may well see something other than the attention to the city or family that virtue might make possible. Aristotle's careful discussion of who should be obeyed in what circumstances cannot in the nature of things reach a rule always to be followed. In sum, proper friendship—friendship as a virtue—is to be with one's own for the right reason, in the right way, time, and place, usually but perhaps not always in the extended sense of one's own, while recognizing the importance of meeting necessity (of advantage) and therefore of the restrictions that one's own puts on choosing friends simply.[5]

Aristotle's discussion of friendship also reenforces our understanding of justice as proper distribution that is based on merit and its link to friendship, as well as the duality of what is natural as the noble but also as (bodily) necessity—what brings into being and preserves as well as what is complete and choiceworthy in itself.

Discussion: The Soul

Aristotle's examination often discusses the soul. We should not take this for granted, because it opposes the view that we can reduce thoughts and actions to their physical or chemical conditions or to psychological factors over which we have limited control. His examination here is not as extensive as in *De Anima*, and he says that he discusses—and the political scientist must understand—the soul only with the precision we need to help secure virtue. From this viewpoint the soul has one nonrational part and one part with reason. Although Aristotle does not examine the soul's varied powers systematically in these works, he does in fact present more than his basic twofold division between reason and what obeys it (or the threefold division that adds the "vegetative power") and the twofold division of reason itself.

Aristotle develops the substance of the part that commands or persuades, which deals with what changes rather than what is permanent, when he examines prudence and the arts in Book VI of the *Ethics*. And he also discusses there the powers of intellect and scientific deduction that can result in wisdom. In the *Rhetoric*, he offers greater detail, indicating the connection between pleasure, perception, and memory. In the *Politics*, as we have just seen, he remarks on the power of our observing likeness and imitation and its relation to what is true. As he says, we are altered in soul when listening to music, and habituation to feel pain and delight in likenesses comes close to a relation to the truth. Indeed, he says that if one delights in contemplating something's image merely for the form, it follows that contemplating the thing itself will be pleasing. And he presents in the *Rhetoric* the general human capacity to learn from examples and follow arguments, although some see conclusions more quickly than others. Furthermore, he differentiates understanding from sense perception while emphasizing the importance and immediacy of perceiving particulars.

As is true of the interplay of goods and passions, we cannot isolate any of the soul's components from what it is oriented to. The soul's work is inseparable from our originally being embedded in certain opinions and practices. It is the source of our activity in directing our passions (one hopes virtuously) and seeing how to meet our necessities, as well as of our activity in understanding what is unchanging as well as what changes. In this sense our actions are primarily those of our soul, and central in our soul is reason and speech: the soul "naturally relates" to beings that differ in kind. It is not encased in a bubble separate from the goods it seeks and the completion for which it strives.

The soul is not a neutral conglomeration of powers because it has a complete, proper, ongoing, mature end, namely, virtue, practical and intellectual. Indeed, it has natural conditions, activities, and motions that are connected to pleasures and their deviations from this to pain.[6] The soul's longings, its desires and spiritedness, can listen to, be persuaded by, or obey reason. These longings thus can be more or less virtuous, but they also have a power of their own, as Aristotle suggests when he differentiates the pride or spiritedness of some from the artistic and thoughtful endowment of others and discusses the existence and, therefore, the need for self-restraint. For the virtuous, the soul's parts are friendly or in order; for others, they are not, and lesser longings may, as it were, treat higher ones unjustly.

The central human goods belong to the soul and not the body, and Aristotle considers the soul among the things most honored.[7] Practical reason deals with what changes, however, so, together with the arts, it is below the reason through which we seek to understand what is permanent. Both ethical and intellectual virtue are choiceworthy in themselves, however, and as virtues of the soul they constitute happiness, as possessed and as active. Aristotle leaves undiscussed the precise relation between what we understand of the permanent and the realm of changeable opinion and action. He also leaves undiscussed the precise relation between observing the changeable political and ethical world and acting within it. I address these issues later. In sum, then, Aristotle's speaking of the "soul" is not an anachronism but a way to characterize complex human action and understanding and its basic, active, source. Discussions of human powers and abilities, of "lived experience," and of our openness to meaning rely on and to a large degree simply rename what Aristotle uncovers in his understanding of the soul.

Chapter Nine

The *Rhetoric*

We turn now to rhetoric, the third major subject of Aristotle's discussions of practice. The *Rhetoric* teaches about everyday speech as such and, more subtly, as philosophy's ground. It too displays Aristotle's ability to show what meets us commonsensically and to clarify it on its own terms. The great bulk of it, from his discussion of the passions to his remarks about the characters of the young and the old, from his discussion of examples and analogies to the major purposes of rhetoric, still rings true. I outline his central points and try to clarify what is obscure in them. Above all, I explore the substance and power of everyday speech, which primarily defines humans and which grounds and makes possible philosophical understanding. The *Rhetoric* makes clear the great practical importance of speech, at least for a community that opens to natural virtue. Speech is not merely a philosophical search for what is true, however; much of what is true is the source of speech that has practical or even playful intention. Although the importance of persuasion points beyond the harshness of political life, moreover, it does not negate it or the presence of force.

Rhetoric, Aristotle claims, is the counterpart to dialectic: both concern what is commonly available and are not themselves distinct sciences with distinct subjects. One can scrutinize arguments methodically, however, and can reflect on why they succeed. Other writers have discussed modes of persuasion but not the body of rhetorical arguments themselves, which Aristotle calls enthymemes. Modes of persuasion may warp the listener as, say, they affect jurors' judgment by causing anger, envy, or pity. The laws should thus define what judges judge, because "it is easier to find one or a few rather than many who are prudent and able to legislate and adjudicate" (*Rhetoric* 1354a36–b1).

Because rhetoric is concerned with rhetorical demonstrations (enthymemes) and these are a kind of syllogism, those who can reflect on syllogisms would be skilled at enthymemes.[1] Indeed, "it belongs to the same power to see both what is true and what resembles truth," and humans "are adequate naturally in relation to truth" (*Rhetoric* 1355a15). Moreover, understanding rhetoric can help the naturally true and just prevail over their opposites, because it is often difficult to persuade scientifically. As is so of all good things except virtue, however, rhetoric can be misused.

Rhetoric, Aristotle continues, is "a power to observe what admits of being persuasive in each case," that is, not as such to persuade but to see the available persuasive points, as an art such as medicine does not produce health but advances it as far as a case admits (*Rhetoric* 1355b27–28).[2] What matters for persuasion is the speaker's character, the listener's disposition, and the speech's establishing something or appearing to. Rhetoric thus is an offshoot both of dialectic and of concern with character, that is, of political science. It is not equivalent to political science, however, but is a capacity for supplying arguments.

Persuading is like dialectics in that one uses syllogisms (enthymemes in rhetoric) and induction (examples in rhetoric). Induction establishes something by referring to "many similar instances," and syllogism establishes that if certain premises are so, something else results, either universally or usually. Rhetoric further concerns what we deliberate about, namely, what can be otherwise, and with signs of this, for example, that fever is a sign of sickness. Moreover, it infers from likelihoods—what happens for the most part—and makes few inferences from necessity. It is not addressed to listeners "who can take a synoptic view of what proceeds through many stages" or can calculate from afar (*Rhetoric* 1357a4–5).

Examples compare a part to a part when they fall under the same class and one of them is more familiar; for example, those who request bodyguards are plotting tyranny. When you are better at selecting topics from a class, however, you "unawares fashion a science different from dialectics and rhetoric," and it is a science if you hit on something's beginning (*Rhetoric* 1358a25). Indeed, most enthymemes come from sciences or semiscientific selection rather than from common topics. Many topics of rhetoric, moreover, do not make you prudent about some class of things but involve general matters such as more and less. Advice concerns what comes into being, not what exists necessarily or begins by nature or chance. That is: we deliberate about what has its beginning up to us and what it is possible for us to carry out. The topics of deliberation, however, do not belong to rhetorical art but "to an art marked by greater prudence and truth."[3]

Aristotle proceeds to discuss the things about which we deliberate and that advisers discuss in public, "things that also leave" their examination to statesmanship. That is, he discusses them only up to a point. The subjects are revenues, war and peace, guarding territory, imports and exports, and legislation. One can gain a synoptic view of revenues from experience and skillful inquiry. Concerning war and peace, one must know one's own and one's neighbors power and how your and their wars have turned out. "For from like things like by nature arise" (*Rhetoric* 1360a6). And one must know territory and sustenance. The rhetorician "must understand what concerns legislation [f]or it is in the laws that the city's preservation lies" (*Rhetoric* 1360a20–21). Moreover, he needs to know regimes and what corrupts them (namely, excessive relaxing or tightening), as well as which are advantageous for "what sorts of people." All regimes except the very best are corrupted by what is their own and by what opposes them. Knowing all this fully is statesmanship's task, not rhetoric's: rhetoric is a power about speech, not about the underlying subject matter.

Aristotle then discusses happiness as the aim of persuasion, the goods related to this end, and, briefly, the substance of regimes. I summarized these discussions earlier.

The ninth chapter of Book I concerns virtue and vice and the noble and base. These are targeted by praise and blame and are central in character (and trustworthiness) and in epideictic rhetoric (e.g., eulogies). The noble is choiceworthy for its own sake, or good or pleasant because of this. Virtue is (said to be) noble because good and praised. It is the capacity to provide and protect good things and to effect all benefactions in everything. (We see that the standpoint here is what others praise, which is sometimes simply and sometimes not simply praiseworthy.) Aristotle then lists nine virtues. Unlike the *Ethics*, he begins with justice, lists prudence and wisdom without distinguishing them from ethical virtues, places liberality after greatness of soul, and leaves out ambition, wit, friendliness, and truthfulness. The focus is on persuasion by pointing out benefactions to others, so justice and courage are honored. Justice involves having what the law says is one's own, not what belongs to others. Aristotle (against the *Ethics*) emphasizes the laws' commands concerning courage and moderation, as he does with justice; he mentions the noble, danger and skill with courage; and he treats greatness of soul as concerning great benefactions (honors are not mentioned here). "Prudence is a virtue of understanding" by which people deliberate well on good and bad things said to bear on happiness. "What produces and arises from virtue is noble and a sign of it." All this is sufficient "for the present occasion"; that is, this is what is ordinarily thought or said about virtue and why it is good (*Rhetoric* 1366b21–27).

"All those for which honor is the reward is noble," as are simply good things one does for the fatherland and less for one's own sake than for others (*Rhetoric* 1336b35).[4] The opposite is what brings shame, and the virtues of those who are more serious are nobler. Justice is noble (even as payback), as are victory and honor. And one honors in terms of what the people one addresses honor (e.g., Spartans, philosophy). With mature men one honors actions that accord with choice, and one takes even chance actions as happening by choice.

In praise, one may amplify: excess here is a virtue. Amplification is suited to epideictic rhetoric (where we are bestowing nobility on agreed-on actions), while examples (judging the future from the past) are suitable to deliberative rhetoric and enthymemes are suited to judicial rhetoric, for the unclear past admits of cause and demonstration.

Aristotle then turns to pleasure, as discussed above, reminds us that people commit injustice for the sake of goods and pleasures, and then examines various just acts in terms of particular and common laws (also discussed above). The standpoint in the *Rhetoric* is injustice as lawbreaking—taking what is not one's own as set by law.

In chapter 15 Aristotle turns to "nontechnical" modes of persuasion, that is, facts to be dealt with rhetorically or manipulated in deliberative and, especially, in judicial rhetoric: laws, witnesses, contracts, (evidence gained by) torture, and oaths. How should they be used when exhorting and dissuading and accusing and defending? So, for example, "it is manifest that, if the written law is contrary to the matter, then one must make use of the common law and matters of equity, on the grounds that these are the more just and is using one's 'best judgment'" (*Rhetoric* 1375a28–31). Written law changes, but the equitable always remains and never changes; the common law also does not change because it "accords with nature" (*Rhetoric* 1375a32–33). Moreover, one can argue that the (relevant) written law is not advantageous and just or that if the meanings of laws contradict one should use justice and advantage as one's guide. Or vice versa: if the written law favors one, one says, for example, that it is harmful to be habituated to disobey authority.[5]

In the second book Aristotle turns to the passions to which the rhetorician might appeal. One must look not only to how the speech "will be demonstrative and credible," which he has been discussing, but to establishing oneself and "rendering the judge of a certain sort" (*Rhetoric* 1377b25). The first is more important in giving advice, the second in judicial matters. As I discussed previously, things appear different or different in magnitude to the angry and gentle, to friends and to those who hate one, and so on. As for speakers being credible, it is because of their prudence (or its lack), their decency or malice (i.e., not giving the correct opinion), and their goodwill or its lack (i.e., not advising at all). Aristotle then goes through the propositions about the passions that I explored earlier.

Aristotle next describes goods that arise from chance that are connected to certain character traits, for example, good birth as leading to love of honor, and he follows this by discussing traits that arise from wealth, for example, arrogance.[6] "For wealth is like a standard of worth of other things and so all else seems to be purchasable by means of it" (*Rhetoric* 1391a2–3). The character trait of someone wealthy is that of a "happy fool," and the character traits manifest with power are similar to those with wealth but better, for the powerful love honor more and are more courageous, are serious, and observe good measure.

Aristotle, having discussed many of the topics of enthymemes, turns now to topics that cover all demonstrations and refutations. The discussion is notable for its references to philosophy and to Socrates. One topic is that all demonstrations should look to the greatest number of facts relevant to the case and not merely be general. Another topic is establishing opposites; for example, if it is good to be moderate it is harmful to be licentious. Another is more and less; for example, if gods do not know all, how could humans? Or if no others who possess an art are base, neither are philosophers. Still other topics are turning statements against oneself back on the speaker, definition (what is a demon? what is arrogance?—examples that relate to Socrates), and the number of ways to understand a term. Still another is induction. For example: "Athenians were happy when they used the laws of Solon, and Lacedaemonians those of Lycurgus, and, at Thebes, as soon as the leaders became philosophers, the city was happy," so philosophers are good rulers (*Rhetoric* 1398b17–19). Another concerns judgments similar to or opposite the point, and still another concerns parts, for example, when in Theodectes's *Socrates* it is asked: "In what temple did he act impiously? Who among the gods believed in by the city has he not honored?" (*Rhetoric* 1399a7–9). Another concerns what follows as a consequence from something and doing this with opposites. Still another is connected to people's saying different things behind closed doors—where the advantageous is praised more—than in the open, where "the just and the noble things are praised." One can thus draw conclusions from one or the other. "This topic exercises a very great authority in producing paradoxes" (*Rhetoric* 1399a33–34). Other topics concern proportionality and "taking what results from each thing as always the same"; for example, "you are going to judge, not about Socrates but about a way of living—whether one needs to philosophize" (*Rhetoric* 1399b10–12).[7] Other topics are people differing in what they do earlier and later; something that could be the reason for something is the reason; inconsistencies; prejudgment; cause, "for there is nothing without a cause"; contraries; errors; and names' meaning (*Rhetoric* 1400a31). "Refutative enthymemes are held in higher regard than are demonstrative ones" because they are shorter, and in both cases people applaud syllogisms that they see from the beginning (*Rhetoric* 1400b25–26).

Aristotle next considers apparent enthymemes (or one might say, sophistry), which are like apparent syllogisms: for example, stating terse or even antithetical conclusions without syllogistic reasoning; equivocating, (falsely) dividing and putting together (e.g., to know the letters is to know the word); exaggeration; illogical signs; and taking as a cause what is not a cause, for example, after something (falsely) means on account of something. And, as in eristics, stating something simply but failing to add "in respect of" or "in relation to what" or "how." So something may be likely not simply but only in a given case but is treated as what is likely simply—as, for example, saying that what is unknown is in fact known or that what is not, is.[8] This apparent likelihood is what making the weaker argument the stronger amounts to.[9]

Aristotle next discusses refutation. In this one constructs "a counter syllogism, or adduces an objection." One constructs syllogisms "from generally held opinions" but many contradict, so it is easy to construct counter-syllogisms. Objections can come from other enthymemes. We state (and can therefore refute) enthymemes on the basis of likelihood (and necessities), examples (where one assumes the universal and reasons to the particular via example), decisive evidence (by showing that an alleged fact is not so), and signs (whether or not they are really so). As I have said, this indicates that, as differing from dialectic, enthymemes do not use their conclusion to uncover or develop premises further but attempt to use premises and examples to reach persuasive results—those that will win the day.

In Book III Aristotle turns to diction. People are persuaded because they are affected in some way, "suppose that the speakers are of a certain sort," or because something has been demonstrated. First, and what I have just discussed, is what makes your subject persuasive. Next is diction, and third is delivery, for one needs to know how to say what one must say. (Voice's relation to the passions, for example, is in volume, harmony, and rhythm.) Justice should be based only on demonstration, but listeners' (and regimes') depravity makes attention to diction necessary. Opinion and imagination geared to the listener matter here but not, say, in geometry.

Aristotle then discusses specifics such as metaphors and similes. To adorn you apply metaphor from better things in the same genus and to blame those that are worse. Metaphors "based on analogy must always be reciprocally applicable and apply to either of the two things of the same genus" (*Rhetoric* 1407a14–16). Metaphors signifying what is beautiful "should be applied from beautiful words either in vocal sound" or, say, in their power of sight. Rosy-fingered dawn is superior to scarlet-fingered or red-fingered dawn (*Rhetoric* 1405b18–20).

Aristotle then turns to correct speech, using specific and not general names for things, not intentionally using ambiguous terms, and so on. Diction also comprises what is fitting "if it conveys the speaker's emotion and character" and is proportional to the subject matter. Appropriate diction makes something credible, for the soul reasons mistakenly that what is being said is true because people are themselves in a similar state. Rhythm too is important: what is without rhythm is unlimited and thus unpleasing and unknowable; "all things are limited by number," and the number that characterizes diction is rhythm (*Rhetoric* 1408b28–29).

After examining other elements of diction, Aristotle discusses "the source of urbane and well-regarded sayings." Producing them belongs to someone with a natural gift or someone who is trained. As with his other discussions of the elements of rhetoric, he uses many political and poetic examples. Words that prompt us to learn something are pleasant, for "learning something easily is pleasant by nature for everyone" (*Rhetoric* 1410b10). One can foster learning through the genus implied in a metaphor—dried stalk for old age, for example. The most well-regarded metaphors "are those based on analogy," and those that make things appear before one's eyes are also well regarded, for these let the audience see what is actually being done, and "activity in motion"—for example, speaking of someone good as one whose flower is in full bloom (*Rhetoric* 1411b25). "In philosophy too, it belongs to someone shrewd to contemplate that which is similar even in things that are far apart" (*Rhetoric* 1412a12–14).

Aristotle continues by discussing diction in writing and arranging speeches. One states the subject matter and then demonstrates it, as if one is defining a problem. Arguing against a charge of slander is especially important, because "all" in the prefaces to their arguments "utter slanders or allay fears." You need to argue against your opponent when he speaks first, for "the soul" is not receptive to one slandered or to your argument if your opponent has spoken well.

Modes of persuasion should demonstrate. One should not seek enthymemes about everything, however, or "you will do what some of those who philosophize do who conclude syllogistically about things that are better known and more trustworthy than are the [premises] from which they speak" (*Rhetoric* 1418a10–12).

Aristotle then turns to interrogation, useful in showing an absurdity, or when it is clear that one point being granted the other will be, as with Socrates's discussion with Meletus about demons' relation to gods, or to show a contradiction. One might counter an interrogation by stating an (exculpatory) cause when an opponent is drawing a conclusion. And, as Gorgias says, ruin an opponent's serious arguments with laughter and their laughter with seriousness. Moreover, some forms of jokes suit "the free human being," and irony is more liberal than buffoonery, because the ironist makes a joke for his own sake, the buffoon for others'.

Aristotle then discusses epilogues. Here, especially, one amplifies or diminishes points made. He finishes this analysis and the *Rhetoric* with his own epilogue: I have spoken; you have heard; grasp it; judge. (That is, there is something rhetorical in the *Rhetoric*.)

Discussion: Rhetoric

Aristotle's discussion of rhetoric is capacious but may not seem to be comprehensive. Has he discussed all types of persuasive speech? On reflection, one can in fact employ his three forms together with his discussion of goods and passions to understand modes that may not appear to fit his three forms precisely.

There is, however, an element of rhetoric that seems to be missing, namely, how deliberative or forensic speakers must often adjust the argument as it is happening to account for its effect on the audience. This involves paying attention to the effect one is having, something that often involves experience. Perhaps general rules exist here, which involve noticing, attention, passion, and reaction. Much of this would concern seeing particulars, but some could be generalized. Aristotle's thought points to the context of this recognition, but he does not work out the elements of ongoing recognition as such. Yet such attention may belong to persuading directly rather than to Aristotle's topic, which is seeing the persuasive points that are available.

Is modern rhetoric different from what we see in Aristotle? Does it build on, or largely dismiss, the phenomena Aristotle brings out? As with the other matters that I have discussed, the core phenomena can be obscured but never fully occluded, and this is so with rhetoric too. Our contemporary judicial rhetoric is stylized or legally professionalized, but this does not prevent basic appeals to passion and justice, and our deliberative rhetoric and advice look to questions of war, peace, economy, and education. The differences with Aristotle largely concern means of technology and the context of liberal democracy, but the purpose and intended effects of rhetoric remain the same. Within our regime, indeed, rhetoric has the odd feature of reducing what is effective in common as opposed to partisan appeal. What the regime means is less taken for granted than it once was. What today can we implicitly take as given, as trustworthy, as common opinion?

Discussion: The Context of Everyday Speech and Trust

The *Rhetoric* allows us to understand more than the substance of passions, goods, enthymemes, examples, and analogy. It also presents the context of everyday speech and comprehension. It shows us the importance of what we first take for granted in thought and action, the importance of speech for establishing this, and speech's limits.

The central context of human activity (in Aristotle but, indeed, simply) involves trust or the dominant opinion in a city or regime about what things are, about what we ordinarily see as goods, about passions as we can arouse them, and about what to expect in deliberative and judicial rhetoric. But it also involves other matters that he discusses in the *Rhetoric*'s second book: the ordinary ability to follow syllogistic arguments, to grasp analogies and examples, and to see matters that are common to all of rhetoric's ends, such as the possible and impossible and what will and has happened. If something is possible, health, for example, one can show that its opposite, disease, is also possible because they belong to the same power. Or one can see that if a genus can come to be so too can its species, and vice versa. And one can appeal to the view that if what is prior to or for the sake of something has happened that thing itself has happened necessarily or for the most part—thunder and lightning, for example. In using examples, one can state what has happened previously or make this up; making up examples consists of comparisons (characteristic of Socratic speeches as, for example, his comparison of choosing rulers and ship's pilots by lot) and of fables. "It is easier to find fables" than to discover past events, Aristotle tells us, "for one must make them up just as one does comparisons, if one is capable of seeing the point of similarity, which is easier to do with philosophy" (*Rhetoric* 1394a5–7). Using facts is better in deliberations, however, because usually what will happen in the future is similar to what happened in the past.[10] As to enthymemes, one should not draw conclusions from steps that go too far back, as the educated do, but one should speak on the basis of opinions marked out in some way (e.g., by judges) as they necessarily or for the most part appear to everyone or to the greatest number.

The central point here is that philosophical ideas are not invented methodologically. They do not come from nowhere or from unfettered production. On the contrary, they belong to or emerge from ordinary understanding of possibilities, causality, examples, time, deduction, and the like. Because Aristotle spells out what the rhetorician should keep in mind to be persuasive, he does not make all speech an inferior version of the fullest philosophical speech. Nor does he trace the path directly from the ordinary intelligibility of, say, cause and possibility to his own understanding. Ordinary speech can be befuddled, as Aristotle indicates when he discusses false syllogisms and sophistry, and not everyone can quickly see the point of a syllogism. The fullest understanding, however, is embedded in or perfects what is ordinary.

Aristotle illuminates the possibilities and context of ordinary speech in the substance of what he says, and he shows, primarily in the *Rhetoric*, how we actually see here and now and the conflicts and imperfections in this. The elements of the human context—what prudence and persuasion must be appealing to, and within, when it is speaking here and now, what is always prior to and alongside any method—become clear. Indeed, Aristotle himself practices rhetoric to the degree that he means to bring one to the position of student or observer or to lead one to see the importance of measured choice, a calm understanding of the variety of claims to rule, how the claim to excel in honor should be a claim to excel in virtue, and how philosophy is itself active, virtuous, and can be useful. Who, then, are we such that persuasion can be effective and habituation to virtuous choice intelligible?

Discussion: Speech and Politics

Let me develop these points. According to the *Politics*, our speech differentiates us from other animals. We can point out or discuss the useful and just and their opposites, while animals have only voice or sound. Speech or reason (*logos*) makes us think of knowledge or science, its deepest use. But here our speech is practical, directed to our choices among changeable matters. We are political animals. Not only do, or must, we meet our needs together; we communicate. Speaking is common or communal and is the central or distinctive medium of our common life.[11]

This leads Aristotle to explicate, primarily in the *Rhetoric* and Book VI of the *Ethics*, the varieties of speech and understanding not only as they are used theoretically, but practically. The *Rhetoric* is from this point of view not a manual of possible actions or treatments, a medical handbook for the attorney or deliberator, as it were, but an explication of the possibilities of speech, the passions and characters on which they can have their effect, the goods to which they persuade, the regime or way of life in which they take place, their musical elements, their degree of generality, and their substantive use of examples and demonstrations. It is here that one sees the substantive connectedness of all speech, theoretical as well as practical. It is primarily in the *Rhetoric*, and in the discussion of prudence, that the place of speech in forming and setting the basic context in which both practical activity and theoretical activity take place becomes explicit.[12] Speech that communicates with others about what is good, useful, just, and beautiful is not meant merely to point out, but to persuade to action. It is therefore connected to possibilities of manipulating and displaying passion and character such that the best or most just result is sometimes but not always obscured. Actual speech in the city, or the community free from mastery, including religious mastery, is, moreover, the medium in which life is lived. It is not merely or primarily a mechanism that, as it were, stands outside of life, even as we are trying to understand speech itself. To the elements of the city (or of the individual) in which necessity is met, force is accounted for, and virtue is to some degree advanced, must be added this general medium in which all activity conducts itself. Speech is the medium of political life, and of life generally, beyond or together, with necessity. Philosophy (dialectic) and rhetoric share this generality.[13]

The context and substance of day-to-day conduct become evident in the *Rhetoric*, including speaking to oneself about the useful, just, and noble. Unlike Plato, for whom all speech wishes to be true or philosophic, Aristotle attempts to show the degree to which we can separate the descriptive and observational from the persuasive. But, as I have said, he is also trying to persuade some of the superiority of the philosophic way of life, to advance ethical virtue, and to adjudicate competing (to a degree, rhetorical) claims to rule. He does and must do this in the basic context of understanding, which is first of all the presupposition, the central trust, opinion, or belief that allows arguments to be grasped and to be persuasive, beyond what is visibly necessary.

Speech, as I have said, is the central medium for political life even beyond but often together with force and necessity. But it is a medium that is not neutral, not merely in its application or even in the substance of what it says, but in the variety of its appeals, mechanisms, and trustworthiness. Everything said is partial: human life swims always in an untrustworthy sea. The fact that speech oriented simply to observing and saying what is true is possible does not change this fact, and the inherent disputability of political things (what is justice, what is greatness of soul, what is the measured action?) exacerbates this difficulty. Stipulation and agreement are necessary politically but cannot fully overcome the maneuverability and variability of speech, the central mechanism of choice and action.

The meaning of these phenomena for our situation today is (among other things) the following: first, the fact that speech is the basic medium of political life and human life in general has not changed and, as long as human things exist, cannot change; second, the fact that speech always occurs within a "regime," a way of life that mixes the noble and the necessary—and, indeed, that speech helps constitute that way of life—also has not and, as long as human things exist, cannot change. The basic elements of political communication (rhetoric) and their manipulability have not varied: the trustworthiness of speech, the appeal to emotions, amplification and downplaying, examples, the basic syllogism, and so on. These are still the heart of both ordinary and extraordinary political speeches and of political advertising. One might say that today our communication can be more visual, more partisan, more selective, and increasingly short, with a growing inability to know its genuine source. Most of these differences stem from our size, political parties, and technology. They do not change the basic elements of rhetoric or the grounds of communication. Complaints about an overly partisan media have in mind a less partisan media in the sense that its presentations are geared to a like-minded understanding of the regime. Concerns about short bursts of information rather than lengthier argument rest on an understanding of what we need in order to grasp complex issues. Concerns about an excess of visual immediacy rest on similar worries. Any attempt at rhetorical or media reform rests on such judgments, alongside a sensible understanding of the inherent manipulability of speech. And, finally, the way that rhetoric's elements—ranging from demonstration to example to commonly understood matters such as before and after and possibility—set the stage for deeper intellectual reflection: this too cannot change as long as human things exist. Such reflection cannot depart altogether from its original context and still remain intelligible.[14]

Chapter Ten

Intellectual Virtue

Book X of the *Ethics* discusses pleasure and intellectual virtue. Its goals are to defend the happiness of intellectual activity in the terms Aristotle discussed in the *Ethics*' first book, to show its superiority in terms of pleasure, and to indicate its limits. In the first chapter he begins with pleasure. As I have discussed this earlier, I start now with chapter 6, where Aristotle returns to happiness. Happiness is an activity choiceworthy for its own sake: it is the end of human concern. It is self-sufficient, moreover, and virtue (as doing noble and mature things) is choiceworthy for its own sake. Play is also choiceworthy but not serious, even if tyrants choose it, for intellect and virtue are authoritative and give "pure and liberal pleasure." Happiness does not equal play (which is childish, and seeks bodily pleasure).

Complete happiness is the activity of what naturally rules and possesses intelligence about the whole and the divine, and it is the virtue belonging to the best. This is intellectual virtue, Aristotle says in chapter 7, and it is the strongest (or best) virtue in us. It is the natural ruler: it is intelligence about the noble and divine and is the divine, or most divine, in us, and it is the most continuous and the greatest pleasure, the strongest about the strongest.[1] Aristotle now calls this intellectual virtue philosophy: it has pleasures that are wondrous in purity and stability. It is also most self-sufficient—the least in need of necessities or of others, even if it is better with others. It differs from action, for nothing comes into being from it, and it is more leisured than politics and war. It is complete happiness, moreover, if one also has a complete life span. Politics and war may be preeminent in nobility and greatness, but war is for peace (except for the bloodthirsty), statesmen lack leisure, and their activity always has an end beyond itself. (These points are reiterated in the *Politics*.) So because contemplation (contemplative virtue) has no end but itself, has self-sufficiency and proper pleasure, and is leisured, it is blessed and complete human happiness. Nonetheless, the contemplative life, although it is divine, is beyond the composite human. Still, we should try to make ourselves immortal and not think only of the human and mortal: we are our own as intellect. Philosophy is the most complete by nature and the most pleasant. The virtues of the characteristically human activities, by contrast, are happiness in a secondary way. Ethical virtue and passions belong to the composite, and the life of intellect is separate. More precision, Aristotle claims, goes beyond his task here.

Theoretical virtue is less dependent than is ethical virtue, for liberal men need money, and courageous ones power. But, the one with intellectual virtue, as a human together with others does choose to act in accord with ethical virtue. Gods, however, do not act with regard to the matters of ethical virtue—not fearing, having base desires, or making contracts. So the height is intellectual virtue—we humans share in this activity, as animals do not—the more contemplation, the more happiness. We need some external goods, however, although a private or measured means and amount is enough for noble action. For this, deeds, action, not mere opinion or "philosophizing," are key.[2] Indeed, if the gods care for us, then it is reasonable for them to care for what is most like them: the intellect is dearest to the gods. Aristotle then turns to the bridge to the *Politics* that I have discussed.[3]

Discussion: Philosophy

Together with Plato's *Republic*, Aristotle's defense here of intellectual virtue or of the philosophic life is the central presentation of its excellence. Aristotle's discussion achieves its power through its elevated restraint and the intentional limits to the precision of his discussion.

Philosophy is a way of life, as Aristotle suggests when he discusses music, not an occasional amusement, a life that is as active, self-sufficient, pleasant, reasonable, and as high or divine as is available to human beings. We should say, however, that in his discussion of intellectual virtue Aristotle does not show (although he perhaps subtly indicates) how our eros and spiritedness are or may be perfected through intellectual virtue. He does not present even the longing for contemplation (as opposed to other goals such as drink, dice, and exercise) as superior in terms of longing as such, and he does not connect wonder, overcoming perplexity, and the dialectical ascent from opinion directly to all the powers of our soul. He treats the philosophical life as divine and pure and as much as possible as separated from our passions. It is the active contemplation of what is highest for and in us. Indeed, he does not examine systematically the elements of nobility or beauty (which characterize virtue) as such. Our composite nature is satisfied with ethical virtue and its attendant intellectual virtue, prudence.

In defending this life and in turning it among other matters to human affairs, Plato and Aristotle initiate an activity that, whatever changes it later undergoes, remains a beckoning and illuminating beacon and a standard for excellence. We should also recognize, however, that Aristotle's indications of the philosophical life in these works go in two directions. First, we see in his discussion of intellectual virtue what the genuine philosophical activity is, broadly speaking, and that it and not merely practical action is a or the human activity. We see some of what philosophy uncovers, beyond Aristotle's immediate political subjects, in his discussion of the soul, pleasure, and what is good. We see this as well in his indications of what the divine might mean rationally, namely, the first beginnings or principles beyond what is merely bodily but not the gods' creation and command. We see it in his honoring of truth above friendship and in his view that "it belongs to one philosophizing" about regimes "not merely to look at action," "but to make clear the truth concerning each thing" (*Politics* 1279b12–16). And we see it in his own procedure of recurring to and investigating as necessary the principles of choice, measure, proportionality, similarity, and so on, going further along the track of ordinary opinion, perception, and perplexities. We see it in the grounds on which he disputes the views of other thinkers.

We also, second, see something of Aristotle's view of philosophy not merely in its own methods and high subjects, but as an activity or way of life in more ordinary terms. At the conclusion of his discussion of friendship he says, "whatever existing is for each, or whatever it is for the sake of which they choose living, it is while being engaged in this that they wish to conduct their lives with their friends. So it is that some drink together, others play at dice together, still others exercise and hunt together or philosophize together, all and each passing their days together in whatever they are fondest of in life" (*Ethics* 1172a1–6). Philosophy is not merely the substantive activity that it is, but a way of life and friendship with the like-minded. It is a proper pastime and choiceworthy for its own sake, but its likeness to others as a pastime makes it familiar and in a sense acceptable. Aristotle downplays throughout the danger that philosophy might present to the community because of its radical questioning and indicates its use for cultivating justice and moderation. He points to this danger, however, in his discussions of Thales, ostracism, and Socrates's trial and in his indications in Book VII of the *Politics* of the superiority of philosophical activity. Philosophy seeks to understand the human good simply and to enjoy a pure pleasure. In its own way it is similar to drinking in its connection to erotic madness and wonder, to exercise and hunting in its connection to spiritedness and overcoming perplexity (finding one's way out of dead ends), to dice (recognizing but sometimes overcoming chance), and to gymnastics (striving to improve or perfect one's soul as one might one's body).[4] Those ambitious in philosophy are said to be angered at those who slight it. In his philosophizing about human affairs, Aristotle presents himself primarily as helpful, moreover, defending virtue, recognizing its ordinary limits in lack of self-restraint, attending to the political claims of the wealthy and free, and reminding philosophers of the importance to them of rhetoric.

Philosophy's central subjects may be the unchanging matters to which Aristotle points in Books VI and X of the *Ethics*, as well as the deepest questions of political or human affairs. But he also mentions philosophy when he discusses how to understand music, how to improve military defense, how to arrange common meals, how to grasp ordinary political life, the opinion of at least some that philosophers may be good rulers, and still other matters. Philosophical activity, moreover, is, together with political activity, the appropriate activity for free men. This suggests "philosophy" as study, observation, or contemplation of many matters and as something other than what is limited only to a very few. In its fullest sense, with its direction to the highest matters, genuine philosophical activity is rare, but it is not directed to these matters alone.[5]

Philosophy also has another ordinary meaning in these works, even beyond Aristotle's likening it to other activities or ways of life. Namely, it is talking about or having opinions about important matters such as virtue rather than acting. (Consider *Ethics* I.) More generally, we can say that the desire to understand, or to have something to say about important matters, or even to overrate the importance of speech, is not a "Greek" invention but is a natural ground of human activity, in its way more honest than our current academic narrowness. Nonetheless, we must distinguish this speech from intellectual excellence. Charlatans too can give arguments, Aristotle reminds us in the *Eudemian Ethics*, so one must also look at and use the phenomena (the evidence) and examples. Even the experienced can be taken in by arguments that seem philosophical, for if one lacks education one is not able to distinguish the relevant arguments from the others or judge when one should distinguish the "through what" (the why, or cause) from what is merely shown. Philosophy is useful in protecting against "philosophy."

Discussion: The Divine

Aristotle as much as possible fits the divine within the natural or makes what is natural "divine." We see this in his use of *Antigone*, in what he says about the common law by nature and sacrifice, in his suggestion that we assimilate the gods' looks and lives to our own (even or precisely if their bodily images surpass us), in his claim that there is something divine in all animals, and in his implicit treatment of Minos. We see it also in his likening elements of philosophy to being godlike and even in his discussion of magnificence and greatness of soul. This is a central question, because if gods do not punish and reward, or if they are not, is there another ground—a natural ground—of what is high? But if gods are not believed to punish and reward, is the natural basis sufficient to uplift or to restrain us? Aristotle tries to deal with this issue, and it is vital for any community. The city and its regime, as the base for all our commonsense understanding, need an orientation to what is at once uplifting and restraining, and in practice this means a broad orthodoxy, even when it is limited by toleration: what we today often call Judeo-Christian virtue. But this orthodoxy should not be so encompassing that it restricts natural excellence. This is why in Aristotle's regimes and in the best regime priests exist but also why they are not independent but belong to the city and are elderly and why he suggests that piety should or need not become silliness.

Aristotle most visibly indicates the difficulties of piety as a threat to intellectual virtue in his use of Socrates's trial in his discussion of rhetoric. Piety in Aristotle is not precisely ours, of course, because of his view of pride as a virtue and humility as a vice and because of our religious toleration. Toleration limits religious warfare (and possible tyrannical domination by a single religion) by making religion essentially private—a voluntary choice. Does it, however, also weaken religion simply? Can human self-elevation—the attention to what is noblest in ourselves—exist properly without passionate yet reasonable attention to what is high? Religion, or belief in gods, that closes or improperly limits philosophical reflection is problematic. So too is the view that traditional exercise of attention to the holy, to what is to be revered in us, is dispensable. We pray for the best or for the conditions that the best requires: the best regime is to be prayed for, and, therefore, a central question is whether we know correctly for what to pray. The gods then act or do not; that is, gods' actions are connected to the results of chance.[6]

Discussion: Statesmanship and Philosophy

The examination of virtue and the arts raises the question of the status of *politike*, of statesmanship or political science. The ambiguity points to the difficulty. What beginnings, or starting points, or principles does political science know or take for granted implicitly? Is it productive or ethical and practical? And what is its relation to philosophy?

Statesmanship or political science is a more general or wider prudence than is prudence for oneself. In both cases one is engaged in obtaining or maintaining goods, so the statesman's concern is among other things the sustenance or preservation of the whole city, the defense of the whole city, and the persuasion that will lead others to choose what is advantageous. But the statesman is also concerned, as is someone virtuous, with the activity of virtue itself. The true statesman or political scientist must therefore be virtuous in order to bring about virtue, or a reasonable degree of virtue, among citizens and inhabitants. Mere cleverness is insufficient. The good man and the good citizen come together in the virtuous ruler. The statesman's completion or end is in his own actions, which, however, also maintain, or make available, or bring about good things for the city and its citizens and, more specifically, justice or the common good, primarily through common defense, common markets, common adjudication of contract and criminal disputes, and, if possible, advancing the conditions for proper distribution and education.

I have just implicitly identified the ruler with the statesman or political scientist. This is not simply correct, for rulers in inferior cities lack full virtue and prudence; their actions will not be altogether just, let alone magnanimous. They may be grounded on their regime's basic premise about justice rather than seeing beyond it but acting within it. We should therefore think of the statesman or political scientist more in terms of the legislator as Aristotle discusses him—not (or not primarily) as an ordinary assembly member within a city but, rather, as a founder or reformer. The political scientist knows what the basic premise is of each regime, how just it is, and what can improve and maintain it. It is unclear or, indeed, unlikely that one could have such knowledge without ethical virtue because of the link between seeing what is just and experiencing or being immersed in the nobility (beauty) one is choosing or attempting to choose. Lacking this, one could not see what fits so that one could attempt to secure it or bring it about. Needless to say, talking with others, including those with less virtue, can enable a legislator to see more, especially of what necessity demands.

This raises the question of Aristotle's own political understanding. He is not a commander or a founder literally, as Solon and Lycurgus are said to be, and is thus closer to someone who merely comprehends and does not command. He is not merely an adviser, however, as someone who comprehends might be. One may consider him an educator or teacher of legislators seen as founders and reformers and even an educator of the rulers, the officials, within a regime who seek to maintain or improve it. His knowledge, indeed, goes beyond that of ordinary founders, as we can see in his one use of the term "political philosophy" and in his deeper discussions of pleasure and what is good than would ordinarily be required politically. His concern, the philosophical concern, is with principles or beginnings, to uncover and observe them, to develop or clarify them with instances or examples and deduction where available, and to connect what is ordinarily said and done back to these principles. In political science this means to uncover the grounds and substance of virtue and then to clarify the chief elements—necessity and the competing claims to rule—from which we judge and construct cities and regimes. It also means that by dealing with these principles but staying on their level and not distorting them, Aristotle can uncover or name things, such as several virtues and vices, the grounds for polities' success, and the importance for virtue of measure and the middle that are not usually noticed or described. Aristotle stays on the path of common understanding but is more farseeing. The one who "philosophizes about statesmanship" "is the architect of the end with a view to which we speak of the end of each thing as being simply bad or good," that is, the true human completion or excellence.[7]

This philosophizing is not contemplation in relation to immediate affairs. Nor is it deductive science. Rather, it is contemplation in the sense of exploring the end of politics—happiness or virtue—such that it can become a trustworthy architectonic end that can guide others. It describes the end (happiness) in terms of its features—goods as noble, as measured, as longed for, and as choosable—explores what makes the end complete (nobility, sufficiency, perfection, and pleasure), and seeks thus to explain what causes perplexities. What is "philosophical" here works up from the ordinary and, as necessary, down or sideways again.[8] Aristotle derives little here from first principles and employs without explaining terms such as "work," "activity," "the natural," and "the simple." He describes matters from the point of view of, and in this sense supplements and in some ways supplants (e.g., in his defense of the superiority of intellectual virtue), the statesman himself as the architect. For as the architect of the end, the one who philosophizes about the political would educate the ruler who commands the bringing about of the end: prudence is not authoritative over philosophy. Even for ordinary arts, it is not the product as such that is the true end but the specifications of the one whom the product serves. And proper understanding of such ends—a beautiful as well as a useful house and furnishings, say—would belong to the virtuous man, or good citizen, as his ends are considered more thoroughly by the philosopher.[9]

To what degree does this mean that Aristotle himself must be immersed in common experience—for our question now, how ethically virtuous must he be? Nothing suggests that the teacher of legislators lacks courage, moderation, liberality, and, even, proper anger. But it seems that he would lack magnificence and magnanimity in their common forms. Yet they are present in a greater view of the honors one might deserve or heights to which one aspires, namely, in the philosophical life and its distance from bodily or useful goods, in its attention to what is divine and beautiful and to the truth (to be honored even above friends), and in its attention to the justice of one's own soul and to the unique friendship of teacher and student. Even if one does not believe that intellectual virtue attends to matters superior to ordinary honors and beauties (although Aristotle surely does), one can see that it allows or does not deny the experience of them. Philosophy, moreover, also seeks sufficiency and purity of pleasure and therefore shares the ordinary concern with pleasure and sufficiency—and, Aristotle believes, better attains it. Aristotle can fully understand virtue either by experiencing it through greater heights or with sufficient attention to others' prudence and actions.[10]

It is useful to contrast Aristotle's understanding of philosophy, political science, and the scope of politics with most current views.

His view of philosophy encompasses today's natural science and mathematics. It is not a narrow discipline, as it has become today. His view of political science follows the political paths of virtue, regimes, and revolution. It does not impose a single mathematical or behavioral method. This connects to his view of excellence in regimes: one regime is not correct everywhere, in every circumstance. His view of politics is not utopian: what is simply good and pleasant is not what all or most choose or what is good in each circumstance. But what is good is not merely what someone desires. Aristotle's political science is not based on, nor does it seek, a single global faith, religion, or divine law. There are unwritten laws that are related to what is natural but no particular divine commands with universal scope. His view of the arts does not reduce them piece by piece to a single universal mechanical or mathematical process or to a single flow of information. The best regime cannot do without intimate acquaintance among citizens: it cannot prosper with merely global communication.

Does this make Aristotle's political science, his statesmanship, obsolete, or, rather, does it again indicate the human base and intentions that give meaning and direction to our endeavors, even technical ones? Philosophy is a human perfection, the basic intellectual virtue, and its goal is truth, things as they are and can be traced to their beginnings or principles (i.e., their completion and fulfillment, their form, what sets them in motion or activates them in their completion or fulfillment, and what sets them in place). Aristotle makes clear that philosophy can aid founders, rulers, generals, and other artisans. But this is not its goal, nor is transformation its goal. For we cannot understand things in their beginnings or principles, that is, what they truly are, if we understand them only as useful, for this makes us see them not as themselves but only or primarily in terms of what they serve. We perhaps especially misunderstand them if we see them only in material or mathematical-material terms. As Aristotle suggests, study of mechanisms of defense and attack can improve attack and defense, but this study does not seem to be based on an understanding of, say, material explosiveness as such. Machines that work independently of human command are easy to imagine, as Aristotle does, but a mathematically grounded understanding of the identity of all motion does not grasp the motions and activities of things in their completeness. One can see how different animals meet similar needs with similar organs, so one might imagine separating or even recombining some of these powers, but, as Aristotle makes clear, one grasps the use and activities of these organs only as part of the whole to which they belong. It is seeing things in their activities, as the whole things that they are, constituted above all by that for the sake of which they are, that should guide any improvement in how we meet our necessities. The always to be repeated attempt to understand, for those capable of this, does not constitute human happiness when it is narrow and specialized.

I have discussed several ways in which technology might, nonetheless, restrict the truth or applicability of Aristotle's discussion of happiness and regimes. Politically, technology affects the scope of speech and of force and their immediacy. The meaning and the proper direction of control, however, are, I have claimed, discoverable from Aristotle's arguments. It is also true that technology's radical possibilities seemingly allow us to overcome both physical limits and human characteristics themselves. This requires us to judge the desirability of how we use our powers. Our ground for judging the worth or harm of such changes, however, belongs to the standpoint of human excellence or completion, for we are judging now, as the beings we are. This standpoint—virtue, ethical and intellectual—begins and perhaps ends with Aristotle's and Plato's discussions—"perhaps" because it belongs to thought to recognize questions whose nature does not allow us to answer them completely. It is also the case that although our modern technology is based on an understanding of mathematically understood matter in motion rather than on Aristotle's view of matter, what we make takes its place in the world of human judgment and use. This is true also of expertise and so-called bureaucratic rationality, whose products and direction necessarily enter the world of commonsense understanding.

Aristotle makes clear that we humans are not gods. We seek to know, but our bodies or our longings limit our understanding. Indeed, deep links exist between ethical and intellectual virtue as a whole. Aristotle asks near the beginning of Book VII of the *Politics* whether a political and active life is preferable or, rather, one divorced from external things, for example, a life of contemplation, "which some assert is the only philosophic one" (*Politics* 1324a28–29). He then claims that contemplation for its own sake and thoughts that are complete in themselves are more active than actions directed to others and for their consequences. For "acting well is the end, so it too is a certain action" (*Politics* 1325b21–22). Moreover, the parts of cities interact (and therefore their actions need not be warlike) as do human beings. Indeed, the god and the whole cosmos "have no external actions beyond what is proper to themselves," and one would not say that they are not in beautiful condition (*Politics* 1325b29–30). And all agree that a happy city is what they believe a happy individual to be. So, Aristotle concludes, "the same way of life must necessarily be best both for each human being individually and for cities and human beings in common" (*Politics* 1325b31–32).

This argument may appear to set the philosophical and the political life against each other or demote practical virtue excessively. On the contrary, I take his argument to suggest that self-sufficiency for the city, and therefore the harmony of its complex parts especially in peace, including the ethical virtue of rulers and their prudence, is what is virtuous and in this way imitates the self-sufficiency and harmony of the cosmos and the god and of true philosophy, in which reason is authoritative and in which intellectual activity involves both acting and the awareness of oneself as acting (understanding). The similarity in happiness arises from the similarity between a just or beautifully ordered city ruled virtuously, a beautifully ordered philosophical soul, and the cosmos and its god.[11] The city is not the cosmos, practical virtue is not the full excellence or beauty of the soul, and the philosophical and political lives will clash. But philosophers are also not gods, nor are they the cosmos, if, indeed, the cosmos is perfectly ordered. (As Aristotle claims, "divine power" "is what holds together the whole itself.")[12] So they too must in their way—as Aristotle does here, or as the philosophers do in Plato's *Republic*, or as Socrates does—take their turn ruling politically and in employing prudence, which is part of intellectual virtue.[13] One might even wonder whether any understanding exists of central principles without humans seeking to know, for themselves. Indeed, knowledge may be inherently limited, or an ordered cosmos never fully discernible, something Aristotle may himself suggest in his view of the variety of categories and their internal multiplicity, for example, the variety in different species of the proper time and place to act and the various meanings of what is and what is good. Does this not indicate a limit to the precise order of things, or to its discernibility, even beyond our composite nature?

Discussion: Aristotle's Standpoint

Another way to examine these issues is to examine what the difference is between a theoretical or philosophical understanding of some realm—politics, music, and rhetoric, say—and the understanding in practice itself. Aristotle uses "theoretical" in these works to mean observing, contemplating, or looking: it is not already to have a "theory" that one applies. To follow Book VI of the *Ethics*, theoretical virtue's fullest goal, wisdom about the most permanent things, is a compound of seen or "intuited" first principles together with "scientific" deductions from them. The first principles are arrived at or developed "inductively," through instances, although it is clear that one must first believe or know something of what a thing is in order to know what exemplifies it and, thus, what its principles are. Otherwise, how might one distinguish what counts as an instance of something from the instance's other qualities—a tree as an example of tree rather than as something brown, green, tall, and so on? For our subjects, which Aristotle examines philosophically but which are not the highest things simply, the first sighting is through trust or opinion. What, then, is involved in the further, observational, developing and looking? One element is noticing and trying to resolve perplexities in a subject and its components. How, for example, given the different views of oligarchs and democrats, should rule be distributed justly? What is happiness's substance? Who precisely is a citizen? What is the most just rule? A second element is to clarify the subject's degree of separateness and independence: Is something merely a useful art, say toolmaking for house building, or is it the complete art itself? A third is to see likeness and similarity: for example, all distribution is proportional; what is good for one species is analogous to what is good for another; and being measured is fundamental in the arts and, by analogy, in virtue. A fourth is to explore systematically—that is, by looking at subjects more thoroughly than do practitioners—what they do or how they have the effect they have, as, for example, what the philosophers do with music or what Aristotle does in the *Rhetoric.* A fifth is to clarify distinctions that are embedded in phenomena but not always spelled out, Aristotle's distinguishing the necessary and the noble in political communities, for example, or his distinguishing what begins by chance, nature, and our choice.

On this basis we can further explore Aristotle's standpoint. By this I mean: At what did he look in finding the general phenomena and descriptions he employs in his thought? What enables one to talk of nature, soul, the simple, virtue, prudence, philosophy, activity, passions, categories, forms, and so on? One factor is his attention to ordinary phenomena and our view of them. Often one can attend to an everyday phenomenon that is already broadly seen, for example, "animals." When necessary this can be the beginning of a more deliberate or theoretical discussion, for example, Aristotle's generic breakdown of animals by combinations of modes of eating, locomotion, and so on. Or one already sees in ordinary life and speech an everyday high and low (gods, the noble, the admirable, pride, some of the simple). Aristotle does not invent this distinction of high and low, nor do philosophers generally. But they explore it. Visible splits exist among species that everyone can notice, as well as the visible existence of the heavens. We deal with or live within everyday time and place. We employ and live within everyday speech (and counting), as I have discussed. There is everyday motion and production. As I have discussed also, Aristotle points to the importance of the mean, the middle, balance, ethically and politically, but he refers this importance to the ordinary experience of its significance in the arts. All this belongs to the general opinions people or citizens have. The key point is that the elements of Aristotle's thought bring out, spotlight, or clarify matters that belong to everyday speech and action. But his observations do not belong to a different realm. His newly named virtues, say, are not unheard-of phenomena. The importance he gives to analogy in discussing being and what is good goes beyond the everyday but in a manner familiar to it. Even his mention of political philosophy in his discussion of claims to rule involves his own balancing of what is visibly contentious. Indeed, he sometimes mentions philosophy itself as, in a sense, ordinarily understood, as he does with music or when he compares it to drinking and dicing.

As opposed to this, when we today attempt to see things methodologically, "theoretically," "philosophically," or historically we often employ much of this standpoint and what is seen within it as an unknowingly taken-for-granted base.

The *Ethics* and the *Politics* and, perhaps especially, the *Rhetoric* allow us to see how Aristotle examines everyday matters in their own terms while also illuminating the phenomena he observes by considering both the intelligibility and the perplexities of everyday activities—what is simple and not simple about something, say, our choice of what we believe to be good, what is perplexing and why. In considering such matters, he discovers the degree of independence of a phenomenon (its partial independence), that is, the wholes or generalities to which it belongs or to which it must belong to be what it is. But because what something is, is to be active in its abilities as it experiences its completion—to be alive, produced, choosing and chosen, thought about and present for thought—the generalities that Aristotle deals with and in some cases elaborates as the correlates of observing or contemplating (causes, beginnings, generalities, categories, activity, powers, to be simply) are also active. That is, they are what they are only as causing, beginning, being a location, quality, or other category, only as active within some aspiration (longing), production, work, and so on. Each choice or action is seen in its own sphere and terms until some perplexity or shortcoming requires it to be seen in broader terms—for example, choices elaborated as measured or noble, arts seen in terms of ends, observing understood as true, clear, adequate, or sufficient. This then allows the philosopher (observer) to see the fuller direction or broader framework of the choice or action (e.g., the true end, the true cause of conflict and relative stability, the broader forms or generalities—genera, time, and other "categories").

When these are discussed one of them may take the lead, for example, what time is or what thought or truth as such is. Theory sees different kinds of things and not only the highest things, or a single being or good. All these terms, even Aristotle's own coinages, such as activity (being at work) or being at work as the end, are connected to the everyday (e.g., work and completion). Aristotle does not, as it were, start from an unformed world and seek to remake it. He begins from our ordinary mature articulation and considers the perplexities, likenesses, and differences in it, including what is there but not as such spelled out. With this, we should return to this book's beginning and to the discussion of Aristotle's political philosophy.

NOTES

Introduction

1. At the conclusion of the *Nichomachean Ethics* (which is followed by the *Politics*), Aristotle calls his work "the philosophy concerning human affairs" (1181b15). My primary goal is to explore the phenomena that Aristotle considers and not directly to address contemporary academic philosophy. References to the *Ethics* without specifying whether the reference is to the *Nicomachean* or *Eudemian Ethics* will always be to the *Nicomachean Ethics.*

2. I also occasionally employ his *Eudemian Ethics* and *Magna Moralia* where they are relevant.

3. See, e.g., *Ethics* 1102a1–5; 1152b1–4; 1181b15; *Politics* 1252a25; *Rhetoric* 1355b27–28.

4. See *Ethics* X, 7, 8.

5. But he does want practice to make a place for philosophy.

6. Moreover, especially in the *Rhetoric*, Aristotle sometimes offers his view without emphasizing perplexities.

7. This is not to say, however, that beings and activities are not ranked. Humans are superior to nonreasoning animals, and intellectual virtue is more beautiful than ethical virtue (see *Ethics* X, 7–9). For discussion of related "ontological" issues, which emphasizes the importance of Aristotle's biological writings, see Thomas L. Pangle, "A Synoptic Introduction to the Ontological Background of Aristotle's Political Theory," *Interpretation* 46, no. 2 (Spring 2020): 261–90. See too Aryeh Kosman, *The Activity of Being* (Cambridge, MA: Harvard University Press, 2013).

8. We may say that Aristotle's procedure is phenomenological in the descriptive sense of presenting what people say or how a phenomenon ordinarily appears while also employing notions that apply to other things as well and

while sometimes bringing out perplexities about the phenomenon that are resolved by showing the resemblance between lesser and fuller versions of it. Aristotle therefore remains with the original phenomena both more and less commonsensically than does Plato, more because he does not so readily develop extreme paradoxes or contradictions to be resolved only by putting a phenomenon on its highest plane (usually or always in Plato the philosophical life) and less because he often describes matters in "metaphysical" terms such as those I just mentioned more explicitly than does Plato.

9. On the issue of Aristotle's audience for the *Ethics*, consider Mary Nichols, *Aristotle's Discovery of the Human* (Notre Dame, IN: University of Notre Dame Press, 2023), 30–31; Aristide Tessitore, *Reading Aristotle's Ethics* (Albany: State University of New York Press, 1996); and for his audience for the *Politics*, consider Thomas L. Pangle, *Aristotle's Teaching in the Politics* (Chicago: University of Chicago Press, 2013), 1–6. For a discussion of this book generally, see Mark Blitz, "To Rule and Be Ruled," *Claremont Review of Books* 3, no. 4 (Fall 2013): 71–72.

10. See *Rhetoric* I, 9, for example, for his more visible holding back.

11. Consider, for example, his discussion of the gods in *Ethics* X, 7, 8. He treats god or the gods as if they exist. God's activity is thinking, however, not creating; it is unclear how much gods care for humans (and if they are multiple, whether they deal with each other); and if they do care for us, or those among us who are philosophical, they do so while lacking the ethical virtues. At the same time, Aristotle suggests the impossibility of men being gods simply while also indicating a divinity and honor in some philosophy that is superior to ethical magnificence and magnanimity, as well as a friendship equivalent or superior to the friendships of the ethically virtuous. Indeed, he suggests that although happiness is complete and self-sufficient human excellence, no actual happiness, no active life, is or can achieve happiness simply.

12. See, e.g., Leo Strauss, *Natural Right and History* (Chicago: University of Chicago Press, 1953); Leo Strauss, *The City and Man* (Chicago: Rand McNally & Co., 1964); Martin Heidegger, *Phanomenologische Interpretationen zu Aristoteles* (Frankfurt am Main: Vittorio Klostermann, 2005) (drafted in 1922), and several of his courses and seminars; Jacob Klein, "Aristotle, an Introduction," in *Lectures and Essays*, ed. Robert B. Williamson and Elliott Zuckerman (Annapolis, MD: St John's College Press, 1985). For a discussion of some contemporary neo-Aristotelianism, see Catherine Zuckert, "Aristotelian Virtue Ethics and Modern Liberal Democracy," *Review of Metaphysics* 68, no. 1 (2014): 61–91.

13. In following Aristotle's lead in presenting the phenomena I discuss, however, I perforce present what I believe to be his view of them.

ONE Happiness, the Good, and the Noble

1. An example of Aristotle's subtlety is that he does not always clarify the structures of the works I am discussing. The *Ethics*, for example, most evidently has two parts, I–VI and VII–X, each concluding with discussions of intellectual virtue, beginning with general discussions of virtue and phenomena close to it, and including discussions of comprehensive practical virtues or a phenomenon close to one—magnanimity and justice; friendship. One might also say that the *Ethics* has three parts: I–IV (virtue generally, the practical virtues, their comprehensive peak in magnanimity, and virtues that point to intellectual virtue—wit, friendliness, and truthfulness); V–VI (a comprehensive practical virtue, justice, and the intellectual virtues); and VII–X. The discussions pick up and elaborate previous discussions, including a circling back in Book X to immortality and the good in Book I and the opening to politics. Connected to this is the fact that Aristotle treats some subjects more than once and not always where one might expect him to. Unraveling this complexity is a challenge. Moreover, his truncated discussions of the soul, of Plato's understanding of the good, of activity, and of other issues are likely to whet some appetites more than others.

2. Because I quote from the *Ethics*, *Politics*, and *Rhetoric*, I mention the work as well as provide the Bekker page number. I also sometimes give a work's book and chapter numbers, e.g., *Ethics* I, 1, or, if the work is obvious, I, 1. I do not generally give Bekker page numbers for short quotations whose location is clear from nearby references.

3. I translate the term *politike* either as "statesmanship" or "political science" (and translate no other term in this way) and translate the term *politikos* as "statesman" or "political scientist" (and translate no other term in this way). I generally follow the Bartlett and Collins translation of the *Nicomachean Ethics*, the Lord translation of the *Politics*, the Bartlett translation of the *Rhetoric*, and the Oxford Classical Texts Greek editions of these works, edited by Bywater (the *Ethics*) and Ross (the *Politics* and *Rhetoric*). Robert C. Bartlett and Susan D. Collins, trans., *Aristotle's Nicomachean Ethics* (Chicago: University of Chicago Press, 2011); Carnes Lord, trans., *Aristotle's Politics*, 2nd ed. (Chicago: University of Chicago Press, 2013); Robert C. Bartlett, trans., *Aristotle's Art of Rhetoric* (Chicago: University of Chicago Press, 2019).

4. I generally translate or refer to *dunamis* and its forms as "power" but sometimes as "capacity" or "ability."

5. The limits to this commanding that Aristotle mentions in Book VI point to what is above politics.

6. *See Rhetoric* I, 7.

7. I translate *kalon* and its derivatives as either "noble" or "beautiful" (and translate no other term in this way).

8. I discuss pleasure more fully below.

9. The fullest good is noble because it is chosen most completely for its own sake and is pleasant, as well as, I may add, being outstanding or rare. Aristotle does not say here why the good of many cities or the world is not preferable to the good of one. I discuss this below.

10. That a close relation exists between happiness and political science, however, is not altogether obvious. Aristotle himself asserts the link more directly in the *Nicomachean* than in the *Eudemian Ethics*. In the *Magna Moralia*, he claims that one cannot act well politically who is not mature (or serious) and that this maturity means having the virtues: ethics is the beginning of political science as a whole, and the discussion of *pragmata* (things that and as they concern us) should be called political, not ethical. Through political science we wish both to know what virtue is and to be virtuous ourselves. And (as we will see) virtue is the substance of happiness. (I use "serious" and "mature" interchangeably to translate *spoudaios*.)

11. The guiding if often implicit standpoint concerning the goods we seek in any regime is a view of the character that is its end and the conditions for whose success we mean to enhance. This character grounds or is connected to the trust, the reliance, the virtuous actions, and other expectations that we require to order arts and productions properly. This is Aristotle's, or an Aristotelian, standpoint, and it is the original standpoint that underlies all political thought and action. Although our liberal democracy loses sight of this, preserving equal rights and using freedom successfully requires certain virtues: responsibility, toleration, industriousness, considerateness, a democratic version of Aristotle's virtues, and practical agreement about certain opinions. I discuss this more fully when I examine the *Politics* and the *Rhetoric*.

12. Consider *Ethics* 1169a23–26.

13. It is unclear what it is for the refined, perhaps an early indication of the similarity for Aristotle between the many's apparent vulgarity and the few's apparent refinement. To be refined (*charieis*) is the ordinary designation for those freed from necessities, i.e., not the virtuous simply. Aristotle does use virtue and being equitable or decent (*epiekes*) more or less equivalently. To be truly decent or equitable is to be virtuous, perhaps especially from the point of view of actions' effect on others, or justice.

14. There is no mention of happiness as piety in the sense of lawful or devout obedience.

15. Aristotle later, in Book X, defends the view that contemplation is an activity.

16. Practical reason is an intellectual virtue, as Aristotle argues in Book VI.

17. This issue has brought forth much commentary. Consider, among others, Ronna Burger, *Aristotle's Dialogue with Socrates* (Chicago: University of Chicago Press, 2008); and several essays, e.g., J. L. Ackrill, "Aristotle on Eudaimonia," in *Essays on Aristotle's Ethics*, ed. Amelie Oksenberg Rorty (Berkeley: University of California Press, 1980).

18. If a complete life were comprised of listening to recordings of Chopin's music, would this life's proper activity be listening to every recording of his compositions, listening to only one recording of each composition, listening to only the best recording of each composition, listening to every recording of the best composition(s), listening to only one recording of each of the best composition(s), or listening to only the best recording(s) of the best composition(s)?

19. Consider the status of Aristotle's own activity here, the variety of his philosophical efforts, which are not restricted to studying the most "divine" objects of "first philosophy," and his claim in chapter 2 that securing the city's good appears greater and more complete than securing an individual's good and is nobler and more divine. Consider too the variety of activities that he calls philosophical in these works (as I discuss later) and his view that the activities that are worthy of a free man are political and philosophical activities. This indicates that elements of theoretical activity are not limited to those fully engaged in it, although such engagement would be the more complete happiness. One may also ask whether we can understand human passions, goods, and pleasures sufficiently without active and presumably virtuous engagement with them. (Aristotle was not an Athenian citizen but came from Stagira, where his father was the court physician to King Amyntas of Macedon. Aristotle tutored Alexander and is said to have been close to Antipater, Macedon's viceroy in Athens.) I discuss these issues below.

For Aristotle's biography generally, see Carlo Naftali, *Aristotle: His Life and School*, ed. D. S. Hutchinson (Princeton: Princeton University Press, 2013).

20. I discuss Aristotle's understanding of the link between virtue and pleasure below.

21. See *Rhetoric* I, 9.

22. Practical reason is an intellectual virtue, as Aristotle argues in Book VI.

23. The bulk of both the *Eudemian* and the *Nicomachean Ethics* is concerned with ethical virtue and allied phenomena such as friendship and self-restraint. The *Eudemian Ethics* has eight books rather than ten, and Books

IV–VI are identical to Books V–VII of the *Nicomachean Ethics*. Both works consider pleasure—but not the way of life devoted to physical pleasure.

24. I use ethical and moral virtue synonymously.

25. See Immanuel Kant, *Toward Perpetual Peace*, Appendixes I, II; *Groundwork of the Metaphysics of Morals*, in Immanuel Kant, *Practical Philosophy*, ed. Mary J. Gregor (Cambridge: Cambridge University Press, 1996).

26. It also deals with the passions of confidence, fear, and anger and their associated goods of victory and vengeance.

27. The emphasis on enjoyment differs from the modern view that the characteristic motion of our souls is restless acquisition, the restless seeking of the means to satisfaction. We see this notion in Hobbes (see chapter 10 of his *Leviathan*) and Locke. Another modern view, that one's goal should be the full use of one's capacities, comes closer to Aristotle's understanding and indicates its continued presence. But the modern view is more egalitarian, having in mind, as it does, one's own capacities without any clear view of the substance and rank of capacities or what using them well involves. And it is also unclear that we understand meeting this goal to constitute happiness. On the relation between motion and activity in Aristotle, see Nichols, *Aristotle's Discovery of the Human*, 46–47.

28. In the *Rhetoric* he discusses virtue and the beautiful more fully in Book I, chapter 9, which concerns epideictic rhetoric.

29. Aristotle will go on to discuss what each of these goods is, although (as he says when discussing a good old age) "the precise account concerning these things is not at all useful for what concerns us at present."

30. Cf., however, *Ethics* 1095b26–27. For an examination of the question of the good, see Hans-Georg Gadamer, *The Idea of the Good in Platonic-Aristotelian Philosophy*, trans. P. Christopher Smith (New Haven: Yale University Press, 1986).

31. In the *Magna Moralia* he adds the better, the soul, the intellect, and the beginnings.

32. Are there largely useless things sought for themselves that are in fact less significant than those sought both for themselves and because of something else? One might think of health as differentiated from a pretty vista or pretty landscaping. But seeing these is not a complete activity.

33. Philosophy may be closer to self-sufficient for oneself than ethical virtue is, and it is a fuller use of reason, but is it more sufficient if family and fellow citizens are taken into account?

34. I use "virtue" and "excellence" interchangeably to translate *arete* (and translate no other terms in this way).

35. See *Metaphysics* V, 16.

36. One may wonder how the end or completion of a lifetime differs from the end or completion that virtue is. We might suggest that our comple-

tion is not length as such but the happiness or virtue that pervades our actions, which fortune may restrict, but which length does not guarantee. As I said, Aristotle does not discuss all the various meanings that "ends" might have—but he does raise the question of whether a short life of noble acts is preferable to a longer, more ordinary one. In any event, neither the ethically nor intellectually virtuous life can escape our mortality. Consider for ends, Martin Heidegger, *Being and Time*, trans. John Macquarrie and Edward Robinson (New York: Harper and Row, 1962), section 48, first published in German in 1927; Mark Blitz, *Reason and Politics* (Notre Dame IN: University of Notre Dame Press, 2021).

37. That is, the unnoticed can allow lying. Consider too the gods' wishes and lying or pretending about them. But see also that the unnoticed causes, although ultimately demonstrable from the noticed, may be the greatest.

38. Consider Amelie O. Rorty, "Akrasia and Pleasure: Nicomachean Ethics Book 7," in *Essays on Aristotle's Ethics*.

39. Aristotle here, and in the *Rhetoric* generally, discusses many topics from an ordinarily convincing standpoint—and, therefore, his discussions are true to a degree. Here, for example, he takes what is usually held to be pleasant and expands it, and he connects it to his view of pleasure as perceptible settling into the soul's underlying natural condition. We should also note how keen his discussion is as practical everyday "psychology" (our term is limited because Aristotle does not, as some do, separate the "inside" from the "outside" in enjoying and knowing)—his grasp of the ordinary and excellent but also the vicious and, as we will see, lack of self-restraint. See too how this view of ruling contrasts with notions of ruling as unpleasant or undesirable "service."

40. This may mean having the virtue of their characteristic activity—e.g., for man, philosophy, and prudence; mere living (which involves their characteristic activity in many or most things); and especially the link between pleasure, reproduction, and preservation of the species, the form, i.e., something not simply material. See *De Anima* 451b4–7. This also indicates a variety and rank of participation in the divine while suggesting that it is not theoretical virtue alone that seeks divinity.

41. Much of the difference between the discussions in Books VII and X derives from the fact that the presentation in Book VII is meant to elevate pleasure from the point of view of the political philosopher as the architect of our end; i.e., it takes the point of view of the political philosopher as statesman. The analyses in my view are at root the same.

42. Aristotle reminds us that Plato has made this argument (in his *Philebus*).

43. The view that virtue is our end leads Aristotle to consider, in chapters 10 and 11 of Book I, the temporal extent of happiness and the place of

fortune in it. It is "activities in accord with virtue" that authoritatively control our happiness. Good fortune helps "adorn" life, but while misfortune may restrict or ruin one's "blessedness," the noble and great-souled bear up calmly under it. The future, moreover is "immanifest to us": someone virtuously active, with sufficient external goods, is happy. Friends and descendants do matter for one's happiness: the considerations are similar to those for oneself. Even if something gets through to one after death, however, it is faint and small and would not affect happiness as such. As I indicated, Aristotle in this subtle way discounts the likelihood of an afterlife that either looks on present activities or rewards and punishes (non)virtuous acts. The finality or completeness of ethical virtue is in the activities themselves and only incidentally in the length of time over which they occur. Aristotle, however, does not deny, nor could he reasonably deny, the status of fortune. Virtue requires sufficient resources; we must meet our necessities, as we may fail to do; and we are subject to the failings of all other animals.

Two The Virtues

1. Someone unrestrained knows what is reasonable (virtuous) but does not follow it; the vicious think that vice should be followed.

2. Longing (or striving), *orexis*, may involve desire, wish, or spiritedness.

3. Consider the *Rhetoric* here.

4. One might say that habit and prudence direct longing to virtue (happiness), except if one naturally longs for this (in which case one still requires prudence). If there is a natural longing for intellectual virtue (happiness), this intellectual activity divinely directs itself (after teaching), but we also require prudence to judge how to deal with our human necessities and goods.

5. See Mark Blitz, *Plato's Political Philosophy* (Baltimore: Johns Hopkins University Press, 2010), 10–15.

6. The Greek term is *hexis*. No translation of this term is perfect if one considers every nuance of English meaning. "Habit" may indicate something rote, but alternative translations, "disposition" or "characteristic," may indicate something inborn, and still others, such as "state," may indicate something fleeting. None of these indications is correct. I use the traditional "habit"; the proper range of its meaning for Aristotle becomes visible in the continuing discussion. But it is also important to see that virtues, and the passions with which virtues deal, orient us in a certain way, so that matters are seen in terms of, say, desire, but concurrently (or, indeed, simply) as desire can be nobly (beautifully) satisfied. Virtue does not stand outside passions but

allows them and the goods that satisfy them to be experienced in a certain way, which then becomes the field within which prudent choice of particulars operates.

7. I use "legislator" rather than "lawgiver" to translate *nomothetes.*

8. Aristotle downplays natural differences in the capacity to become virtuous, but they are indicated at 1103a25.

9. Presumably, a truly artistic deed also requires that one has the art and does not merely achieve an artful result. The product is separate from the producer, however, in a way that a virtuous act from a virtuous character is not.

10. It is significant to note both the shortcomings of this ordinary sense of "philosophizing" and the indication that proper philosophizing may be sufficient for intellectual virtue, which is the higher virtue. I discuss Aristotle's various mentions as well as his discussions of philosophy in these works in due course.

11. In the *Rhetoric*, however, he mentions only one vice as the opposite of a virtue (*Rhetoric* 1366b13–20).

12. We should note that this discussion makes clear that happiness is not an ordinary but a rare human accomplishment, as opposed to our contemporary view.

13. "Ethical" virtue derives from *ethos*, the Greek term for "character."

14. The central later question should be whether, while not ignoring or distorting the ground that Aristotle uncovers, one sees shortcomings in his understanding.

15. See the discussion of magnanimity in Book IV, of justice in Book V, and of intellectual virtue in Books VI and X.

16. See, among the many discussions of this issue in Aristotle, T. H. Irwin, "Reason and Responsibility in Aristotle," in Rorty, *Essays on Aristotle's Ethics.*

17. Consider how Book III begins with reference to legislators.

18. To translate *pros* in this context, I use the neutral "related" to ends rather than "conducive" to them or "means" to them because what we choose as related to an end may be a constituent or element in it and not a means to it or otherwise subordinate to it.

19. I discuss what Aristotle means by "the simple" below.

20. What makes a good truly noble and pleasant? One may say, its completeness, perfection, and sufficiency, as Aristotle discusses this with virtue: complete and perfect human activity. Given Aristotle's discussion of the soul here, however truncated, this completeness would need primarily to involve reason, as knowing and as commanding and being listened to. Thus, intellectual virtue and the good for which it longs (strives) is primary, and the height

of an ethical virtue depends on the height, or nonanimality, and comprehensiveness of the goods with which it deals and how much they can be rationally directed (through the scope of prudence and the just proportions of a regime) beyond merely animal necessity.

21. Several elements of Aristotle's discussion of virtue up to this point are clarified or expanded in the relevant sections of the *Eudemian Ethics*. All substances, he tells us, are by nature beginnings (principles) and can therefore generate many suchlike things, e.g., men from men, animals from animals, plants from plants. Strictly, men alone generate actions, and these are beginnings strictly—even more so are those with necessary results, e.g., the gods. This authoritative sense of beginning does not belong to things incapable of moving, e.g., mathematical things, although by analogy we say it, because to change the principle (axiom) is to change what is proved from it. But they do not change themselves. Man is a beginning of motion, and action is a motion, and the beginning is a cause of what comes into being, as a triangle having two right angles means that a quadrilateral has four. What depends on men may or may not happen, and goodness and badness have to do with things that we cause. We deliberate until we carry the starting point (in bringing us the end) back to ourselves. Longing is deliberative when its beginning or cause is deliberation. The conclusion: choice is opinion plus longing when choice follows as a conclusion from deliberation.

22. The key point here is that the passions affect the way the evidence that might make a speaker credible is taken or comes to light. Passions color or even help form the context of understanding, and this is connected to the fact that they are amenable to speech.

23. *Rhetoric* 1379a35.

24. "It is impossible to feel fear and anger simultaneously" (*Rhetoric* 1380a33). Consider, for fear, Heidegger's *Being and Time*, section 30.

25. Consider Socrates's discussion with Cephalus in the *Republic*.

26. See *Rhetoric* II.

27. In this section I intersperse my comments about Aristotle's discussions with my summaries of them.

28. For a discussion of Aristotle's understanding of courage, see Lorraine Smith Pangle, *Reason and Character* (Chicago: University of Chicago Press, 2020), 104–22. For *Reason and Character* generally, see Mark Blitz, "Happiness and Honor," *Claremont Review of Books* 22, no. 4 (Fall 2020): 98–99. For the ethical virtues generally, see Susan D. Collins, "The Moral Virtues in Aristotle's Nicomachean Ethics," in *Action and Contemplation*, ed. Robert C. Bartlett and Susan D. Collins (Albany: State University of New York Press, 1999).

29. Consider Plato's *Symposium*.

30. Consider Plato's *Statesman* 306e1–12.

31. In various ways he expands the field of his discussion but subtly and not in all cases. For Aristotle in relation to Plato/Socrates, see especially Burger, *Aristotle's Dialogue with Socrates.*

32. The fitting and the great, outstanding, admirable and rare link, in different degrees, ethical and intellectual nobility. Consider, for example, the references to wonder.

33. See 1124a18; See too *Eudemian Ethics* III, 5. The term for "honor" and "office" is the same—*time*. Honor as office is not used often in the *Ethics* as opposed to the *Politics*. But see 1134b7 and1168b30. Much of Aristotle's effort is to turn seeking honor to seeking honor for being virtuous.

34. See especially *Politics* III.

35. One should consider here the character and aspirations of Washington, Lincoln, and Churchill.

36. Consider among other discussions of greatness of soul, Nichols, *Aristotle's Discovery of the Human*, 99 ff.; Burger, *Aristotle's Dialogue with Socrates*; Jacob Howland, "Aristotle's Great-Souled Man," *Review of Politics* 64, no. 1 (2002): 27–56.

37. We will see later in the *Ethics* a connection between spiritedness and friendship and rulers and friendship. We might also suggest that, after courage, the other virtues mimic Plato's three classes and divisions of the soul, three virtues for each, with the emphasis on spiritedness.

38. In Book III of the *Eudemian Ethics* Aristotle turns to specific virtues. I indicate what adds to points made in the *Nicomachean Ethics.* Some things are fearsome simply, others only to someone. What the coward as coward fears is not fearsome to everyone or only slightly. Things that are fearsome to most are said to be fearsome simply. These are fearsome to the courageous as human beings but not, or hardly, as courageous. Reason tells us to choose the noble, so enduring the fearsome through recklessness or being out of one's mind is not noble courage. Moderation is truly about touch, and all by nature enjoy (and desire) things that almost all share in. Animals' pleasure is in taste and touch but not the other pleasures, even when their senses are keen. They are not affected by beautiful sights and sounds except through an accidental marvel. Gentleness (proper anger) is about the pain from spiritedness. The harsh feel too quickly and for too long and in the wrong time and place. Greatness of soul, magnificence, and liberality are middles, where "ought" means according to right reason. Liberality involves acquiring and spending wealth. The great souled are concerned not with ordinary honors but with offices and other goods that are truly great and conferred by the few. Each virtue seems great souled in regard to its good. (This is one reason that the great souled seem to have all the virtues.)

Magnificence is what is fitting in ornament. The fitting (e.g., in weddings or embassies) is the suitable, as reason directs—fitting in relation to each particular, e.g., servant, favorite, self. (One should note as well the different order of the discussion from that in the *Nicomachean Ethics*.)

Aristotle then discusses several matters somewhat differently from his discussions in other works, in particular, other middling states that are not virtues, for they do not involve choice: they are praiseworthy passions. These are not virtues, but they are natural, and they contribute to the virtues; i.e., they contribute to what follows thought. Nemesis (indignation) contributes to justice and envy to injustice, shame to moderation and truthfulness to wisdom.

39. One might also consider loyalty, not on his list or especially democratic, but in a sense accounted for in his discussion of friendship. I discuss our democratic virtues further below.

Three Justice and Prudence

1. In the section on justice I usually but not always intersperse my comments about Aristotle's discussions with my summaries of them.

2. Consider here Burger, *Aristotle's Dialogue with Socrates*; Nichols, *Aristotle's Discovery of the Human*; Pangle, *Reason and Character*; Bernard Williams, "Justice as a Virtue," in Rorty, *Essays on Aristotle's Ethics.*

3. That the same thing (here virtue) differs in being seems to mean that it differs in extent, or in relation to different categories. Something's full being would be its complete activity. Consider *Metaphysics* V, 7.

4. This question will become a theme of Book III (as well as Book VII) of the *Politics*. See also Book X of the *Ethics*.

5. This is another theme of the *Politics*.

6. I discuss these matters more completely when I turn to the *Politics*.

7. Consider *Politics* III, 12.

8. This is the necessary not as differentiated from the noble but as unable to happen any other way.

9. We should notice how Aristotle here describes how chance looks commonsensically but also points to the definition given in *Ethics* I, 5 in *Physics* 195b ff.

10. *haplos* (simple) and *physis* (nature).

11. See *Ethics* VII, 14; VIII, 4; IX, 4.

12. As I have indicated, the simple as what is unmodified can be or can point to what is excellent—someone who can judge simply and not only about one thing, for example, or what can be known simply and not only to us (See *Ethics* 1095a1–2 and 1095b3–4). It can also point to a limit or an imperfection,

however, as ordinary or usual law simply can be improved in its just application by equity. Indeed, in the *Rhetoric* the simple can be the simple-minded.

13. The natural as essential, as what something is, can therefore be the universal, or what is rarely completed. The universal end of plants and animals is the reproduction of their species and being alive or active in their form: species differ in the perception and nutrition connected to this, but individuals and groups within these species vary only marginally if at all. The freedom required to reach our human end, however, means that the way that we deal with our natural or universal necessities varies economically and politically.

14. See, e.g., *Ethics* 1135b4; *Ethics* X, 7, 8; *Politics* I; *Metaphysics* V, 4.

15. In this section I intersperse my comments about Aristotle's discussion with my summary of it.

16. Brasidas was an important Spartan general, discussed by Thucydides in his *History of the Peloponnesian War*.

17. See also *Ethics* II, 1. On the question of natural justice in Aristotle, consider Strauss, *Natural Right and History*, 156 ff.

18. See *Politics* VII, VIII.

19. Even the substance of virtuous actions varies: virtue is as the prudent man chooses, but these choices are not mathematically exact.

20. *Rhetoric* I, 13. (Quotations here are from this book and chapter.) One might translate "common" here less literally as "general" to avoid confusion with, say, the British common law.

21. *Rhetoric* 1374b1. Written dictates are "marked by necessity," while the unwritten are not. "Better" people are just without the necessity to be so.

22. Notice how Aristotle naturalizes the divine. See Bartlett's commentary on this discussion in his translation, pp. 243–45.

23. See *Ethics* VIII and IX on friendship; and *Politics* III.

24. Consider Book X and philosophy generally. I am not discussing here another way that natural justice can be changeable, namely, the ways in which our two natural ends, ethical and intellectual virtue, may not be fully compatible. The Socratic is small souled politically, for example, and radical in his questioning in a way that the community cannot be. But this is not to say that a good regime cannot in practice advance both. I discuss Aristotle's own justice below.

25. Is equity connected to the laws and justice of a particular regime, or is its standard full natural justice? In the *Magna Moralia* and the *Rhetoric*, equity seems to have in mind a natural standard. Perhaps we may say that equity attempts to correct any city's laws in the direction of natural justice but that equitable acts in similar situations might therefore vary according to a city's regime.

26. Consider Plato's *Republic*, Book IV.

27. Here and in other places in this chapter "characteristic" may seem more appropriate than "habit."

28. *Ethics* 1140b5–6.

29. What is the status of Aristotle's own knowledge here—his distinguishing modes of truth? I discuss Aristotle's standpoint below.

30. Being here, again, is what something covers, or what it is in relation to, which may involve different categories but does not here. As the same habit (or characteristic), it is the same work or power.

31. For they may see universals as well as particulars. See too the various times of life mentioned here: understanding nature has something to do with age as well as with intellect simply.

32. This and earlier references indicate that producing is not limited to making things that stand altogether outside of the action, although this is the usual or primary meaning. Fundamentally assimilating practice to production is a feature of Martin Heidegger's understanding of Aristotle. One might consider, for example, the summaries of Heidegger's seminars on Aristotle in the 1920s that were preserved by Helene Weiss and have now been published in Francisco J. Gonzalez, *Human Life in Motion* (Bloomington: Indiana University Press, 2024).

33. See too *Ethics* VII, 10. In the *Rhetoric* Aristotle says that the character of someone prudent resides in pursuing advantage, while that of someone good resides in pursuing the noble. In the *Ethics* he amends or elevates this common view so that prudence also or primarily concerns virtuous or noble action.

34. Aristotle continues his discussion with Socrates, as it were, about the connection between knowledge and virtue in Book VII. See Burger, *Aristotle's Dialogue with Socrates*.

35. Might prudence also suggest when the philosopher should speak or act politically and when he should be cautious?

36. Aristotle's view of prudence has occasioned much discussion, especially concerning whether prudence concerns what helps constitute virtue rather than choosing means to it and the way in which prudential thought is syllogistic. Many of these often illuminating discussions do not consider sufficiently the meaning of the beauty of virtue or the question of statesmanship. Consider, among others, Carlo Naftali, *The Wisdom of Aristotle*, trans. Gerald Parks (Albany: State University of New York Press, 2001); C. D. C. Reeve, *Aristotle on Practical Wisdom* (Cambridge, MA: Harvard University Press, 2013); and several of the articles in Rorty, *Essays on Aristotle's Ethics*, e.g., David Wiggins, "Deliberation and Practical Reason."

37. See, e.g., *Ethics* 1119b16 and 1138b22.

38. My discussion of the connections among the passions, goods, and regimes raises the question of whether there is a true whole within which expe-

rience occurs. What one can say, with Aristotle, is that there is, as goods and passions belong together with and come to light for the noble and virtuous (including their justice), the ones for whom the good and pleasant is what is good and pleasant simply. And such noble activity is a fullness or completeness, a being at work in the end, where each action is an instance or element of this excellence or stems from it. For us humans this is ultimately more theoretical than practical because of philosophy's being guided by the intellect and being oriented to first principles. I discuss Aristotle's understanding of the connection between practical and theoretical virtue more fully near the book's conclusion.

39. As I said earlier, one may translate *politike* as "political science," as I sometimes do—but this may lead us to think of this knowledge as an art or science, i.e., as separate from action. Some elements of it, however, may differ from action directly, let alone from production: it is architectonic. "Statesmanship," the other translation I often use, is usually the most sensible one, as long as one does not identify it with a meliorating or compromising disposition.

40. One might also suggest that the founder's perspective may require Aristotle's own knowledge or be directed toward what he discusses. When is it necessary to know what virtue is—a habit, not other qualities of soul, measured, not mathematical knowledge—beyond having good character and the prudence connected to this? Aristotle's "political philosophical" knowledge goes beyond or is different from prudence itself. See also Aristotle's remark on being the architect (*Ethics* 1152b2) and the *Politics* overall but especially Books VII and VIII. I discuss this issue more fully below.

41. Consider here my discussions of prudence as seeing what is fitting.

Four The City and Its Necessities

1. On the relation of the *Ethics* and the *Politics* to "contemporary problems," see, however, Eugene Garver, *Aristotle's Politics* (Chicago: University of Chicago Press, 2011), 14–15. The chief question with the structure of the *Politics* is whether the discussions in Books VII and VIII were in fact intended to follow Book III. Lord examines the relevant issues in his introduction to his translation.

2. Consider what this indicates about the human origins of gods.

3. *Chrematistike* can also be translated here as "getting goods" or the "science of getting goods." I translate it, and only it, as "provisioning," "getting goods," or the "science of getting goods."

4. Consider here Plato's *Greater Hippias* 289a1–d5.

5. See *Ethics* VI on stewards.

6. For several of the questions covered here, see Abram N. Shulsky, "The 'Infrastructure' of Aristotle's *Politics*: Aristotle on Economics and Politics," in *Essays on the Foundations of Aristotelian Political Science*, ed. Carnes Lord and David K. O'Connor (Berkeley: University of California Press, 1991), 74–11.

7. As I said, nature includes for Aristotle what we do not make.

8. There is no discussion of a use of capital (and the interest paid to borrow it) for continued investment, as differentiated from its possible use here to help secure a monopoly.

9. "Authority" here does not mean men's physical strength but the dominance of reason over passion.

10. This may seem to differ from Plato's *Republic*, where the regime controls lesser communities. But as Aristotle has just said, the household and its parts belong to the political whole. In inferior regimes relations in these parts all become or tend to become democratic or oligarchic.

11. Also consider the so-called city of pigs, the "true" city, outlined in the second book of Plato's *Republic*, and Plato's discussion in the *Statesman* 264d1–266c1.

12. Consider the connection between spiritedness and friendship that we will see in Aristotle's discussion of friendship.

13. Perhaps it is even a justifiable but not exclusive imperialism. Consider the discussion below of Aristotle's examination of intellectual virtue in *Ethics* X.

14. For several of these issues, consider Shulsky, "The 'Infrastructure' of Aristotle's *Politics*"; Stephen G. Salkever, "Women, Soldiers, Citizens: Plato and Aristotle on the Politics of Virility," in Lord and O'Connor, *Essays on the Foundations of Aristotelian Political Science*, 165–90; Judith A. Swanson, "Aristotle on Nature, Human Nature, and Justice," in Bartlett and Collins, *Action and Contemplation*; Wayne Ambler, "Aristotle on Nature and Politics: The Case of Slavery," *Political Theory* 15, no. 3 (August 1987): 390–410.

15. See *Politics* 1330a32–33 on freedom as a reward; and *Ethics* 1161b6–9 for the slave as a human being and not only a slave.

16. For a discussion of Aristotle's intention to more fully develop a discussion of the connection of virtue and education to particular regimes, see Paul A. Vander Waerdt, "The Plan and Intention of Aristotle's Ethical and Political Writings," *Illinois Classical Studies* 16 (1991): 231–53.

17. With regard to the connection between character, goods, and passions, we again see that one cannot describe passions and character properly without connecting them to goods and then to the better experience of, and dealing with, these goods. For goods to be experienced as goods they carry their evaluation—and perhaps, their simple evaluation (and for Plato, their fullness) with them.

18. *Rhetoric* 1389b10.

19. See *Politics* 1336b3–6.

20. Note the height of magnanimity here and the link between magnanimity and freedom.

21. *Politics* 1340a17.

Five The Regime

1. For the discussion in Book II, see Richard Bodéüs, "Law and Regime in Aristotle," in Lord and O'Connor, *Essays on the Foundations of Aristotelian Political Science*.

2. *Politics* 1264b18–22.

3. Aristotle's discussion here is more about the laws than the regime, which he believes is Sparta's regime, and where he says the education is the same as in the *Republic*.

4. For an extensive discussion of Book III that among other issues emphasizes the question of wholeness, see Delba Winthrop, *Aristotle: Democracy and Political Science* (Chicago: University of Chicago Press, 2019).

5. Consider here the link between offices and honors to understand how magnanimity involves political office as an honor. Honor for virtue is central, but virtue fully and prudence fully require being able to act, that is, require political rule. The magnanimous man might also wish to be treated as a god or even a king simply, but this would be vanity, not greatness of soul. Lower or false honor would be for, say, great wealth. And as Aristotle makes clear, all political offices must not go to those most virtuous simply. The philosopher might be honored by other knowers for his intellectual virtue, but this is not what he seeks.

6. That is, better in, say, looks by a margin larger than the other is better in flute playing.

7. Consider my discussion of distributive justice in *Ethics* V.

8. Consider my discussion of the *Rhetoric*'s account of unwritten law.

9. This is then discussed in Books VII and VIII.

10. The word for types of persuasion—*pisteis*—is connected to the word for trust—*pistis*.

11. See Locke's *Second Treatise*, section 89.

12. This is not to say that attention in Aristotle to matters of character that are not simply encapsulated politically is insignificant. Consider philosophical activity and what Aristotle says in the transition to the *Politics* at the end of the *Ethics*.

13. Consider Plato's *Gorgias* 491e5–495b1.

14. For further discussion, see Mark Blitz, *Duty Bound* (Lanham, MD: Rowman and Littlefield, 2005), 7–24; Mark Blitz, *Reason and Politics*, passim.

15. For a discussion of Locke's understanding of desire and pleasure, consider Mark Blitz, *Duty Bound*, 145–65.

16. See Harvey C. Mansfield Jr., *Taming the Prince* (New York: Free Press, 1989), chapter 6.

17. See Leo Strauss, *On Tyranny* (Ithaca, NY: Cornell University Press, 1968); Mark Blitz, *Reason and Politics*, 178; Mark Blitz, "Tyranny Ancient and Modern," in *Confronting Tyranny*, ed. Tovio Koivukoski and David Edward Tabachnik (Lanham, MD: Rowman and Littlefield, 2005), 9–24.

Six Regimes

1. He discusses this last issue primarily in Book V.

2. Note the importance of proportion. Nature here means what is required for something to come into being lastingly.

3. Some differences, e.g., whether ruling offices are those that deliberate as well as command or primarily command, make no difference in use, he says, but merit thought.

4. See *Politics* 1339b5.

5. For the issue of the relation between equal individual natural rights and natural excellence, consider Blitz, *Reason and Politics*, passim.

6. This makes clear how rare full virtue is, even accounting for the possibility of those who are virtuous but lack "high birth."

7. Compare the discussion of magnificence in the *Ethics*.

8. *Politics* 1309a33–39.

9. I consider the range of Aristotle's understanding of persuasion when I discuss his *Rhetoric*.

10. We should also note that the commonality of unwritten (or natural) beliefs is a kind of (humane) check on cities.

11. Indispensable need not mean sufficient, and I discussed above the question of liberal democratic regimes based on equal natural rights and the meeting of necessities and, therefore, the justice and understanding connected to the revolutions that bring them about.

Seven Political Excellence and Its Limits

1. *Politics* 1322a7 ff.

2. Note the limited place of priests and the importance of arms.

3. *Ethics* 1140b14.

4. For a discussion of self-restraint (or as she translates *akrasia*, "lack of self-control"), see Pangle, *Reason and Character*, chapter 6.

5. *Rhetoric* II, 6

6. The god, however, he says, is happy not through external goods but by being of a certain nature.

7. See also *Politics* 1328a1. I discuss these statements below in examining the understanding of philosophy that becomes evident from these works.

8. See also the discussion below of friendship in the *Ethics*. One might thus distinguish friendship and erotic love, where eros is a reaching out and gazing at, but spiritedness is protection of—love of—one's own.

9. See also *Metaphysics* 1029b3–9.

10. Flutes are for intense, even cathartic feeling, Aristotle suggests, but not for learning. (And they prevent speaking.) Athena, according to myth, invented flutes but threw them away as they "have nothing to do with intelligence," and "we ascribe to Athena knowledge and art" (*Politics* 1341b8–9).

EIGHT Friendship and the Soul

1. One might say in general that the primary and authoritative version of a thing is the thing in all respects—here friendship of the virtuous—and that the others have it in some respects but not in all respects and not fully, for example, in friendship, being together with others for some good but not the true good, not always being with each other, seeking (in utility) to be benefited more than to benefit (and seeking ordinary pleasure), etc. A universal definition would be too empty, and one that merely left things at the best would be too restrictive. In Plato, by contrast, we have eros directed to the true thing and the different circumstances or materials in which there is an image or reflection of the true thing.

2. But is it also the case that the friend here is more worthy? If so, there is no issue, as there is not in aristocracy, for even if one is a bit superior the regime benefits from rotation. The issue for the city and in a way oneself would be if one were very much superior. Or does this difference also have in mind philosophy—the more noble—vs. politics, where one gives up politics for philosophy?

3. Aristotle also discusses friendship in Book VII of the *Eudemian Ethics*. Much of his discussion is similar to that in the *Nicomachean Ethics*, so I will mention only a few matters. The goal of the discussion, he says—and this is central generally—is to find a logos that agrees with the phenomena and can, when the contradictions and perplexities are shown, show the reason in them, i.e., that they are true in different respects.

One seeks that the good simply is good for oneself, and one should avoid bad things, but good for oneself and simply may differ. The simply good is choiceworthy, and the good for oneself is (choiceworthy) for oneself: they should agree, and virtue makes this so. Statesmanship is for generating this when it is not so.

In chapter 12 Aristotle turns to perplexities of self-sufficiency and friendship. The god does not need friends, and the self-sufficient have few, but they are with virtue and to share our enjoyments. Life is perception and knowledge. This is most choiceworthy individually, and therefore nature puts in all a longing to live. Knowing itself, according to itself, would mean no difference between myself and another's knowing, i.e., living. But knowing/perceiving (for) oneself is reasonable and more choiceworthy. One wishes always to live because one wishes always to know because one wishes to be the object known (i.e., self-consciousness but not in the modern sense where self-certainty is the ground of truth but, rather, knowing oneself as knowing). So is a friend another self? By nature a friend is most akin, but different friends resemble one in different ways. Still, a friend is, as it were, a different self. To know and perceive him is to know oneself, and one especially shares the divine pleasures and contemplates oneself enjoying the better good. The god's excellence is such that he thinks of nothing other than himself as himself: he is his own well-being.

4. Aristotle does not discuss the differences among the various terms he uses for love and friendship. Friendship is the basic term, so he can also use it for the others.

5. Consider here Aristotle's linking of spiritedness—which defends oneself, one's city, and one's family—to friendship in the *Politics*.

6. *Rhetoric* I, 11.

7. Statesmanship and prudence do not rule over the gods, wisdom, or the soul's better part, as medicine does not rule health.

Nine The *Rhetoric*

1. Are enthymemes identical to dialectical syllogisms but differently named merely because of their rhetorical context? We may say that enthymemes are syllogisms that are meant to persuade rather than to find the truth. As is true of dialectical syllogisms, they do not begin from (simply) true first principles: they are not scientific but start from opinions. Unlike a dialectical search, however, they are not intended to clarify the accuracy of the premises from which they begin or to help reach first principles. This difference would also characterize the difference between induction and rhetoric's use of examples.

2. We might suggest, however, that the difficulty is greater in rhetoric, for despite the help Aristotle might give in preparing speeches, it can be difficult to address a complex and divergent audience, to know its passions or to know which argument would work best at the time. One often knows one's audience less well in rhetoric than one does one's patient, or usual patient, in medicine, and the situation may change more rapidly in the midst of one's discussion because of reaction to what one is saying, opposition to it, and real or perceived change in the circumstances.

3. Knowing what is truly advantageous belongs to statesmanship.

4. This obscures virtue as one's own nobility or happiness. Here one is showing the character and recommending the measures that will lead others to choose a certain way.

5. See my discussion in chapter 5 above of Aristotle's view of Hippodamus.

6. The virtue of a family line, he reminds us, may degenerate "from its nature," and there may be extraordinary men who degenerate into crazy characters, e.g., those descended from Alcibiades and Dionysius the Elder, and stable ones who descend into "stupidity and sluggishness, e.g., "from Cimon, Pericles, and Socrates." Consider here also Plato's *Statesman* 307c1–311a2.

7. What accounts for the emphasis on Socrates? Most visibly, it defends Socrates and the philosophical life while also indicating philosophers' need for rhetoric. It also shows the utility of philosophy as a source for discovering modes of effective rhetoric. Does not rhetorical speech ultimately point to or depend on knowing the truth and to knowledge of goods, passions, and character, i.e., here, to Aristotle?

8. Consider several of Plato's dialogues, the *Meno*, *Parmenides, Sophist*, and *Euthydemus*, for example.

9. The prevalence of apparent enthymemes does not affect the point that all enthymemes are meant to persuade, i.e., not as such to pursue full truth. When the enthymeme is not apparent it employs correct reasoning from a generally held but not necessarily altogether true or relevant opinion, e.g., an accepted opinion about justice.

10. Consider here Aristotle's own use of examples from both poetry and fact and his concluding statement.

11. *Politics* 1253a9–15.

12. See also Aristotle's *Organon* but not for the phenomenon of context.

13. They also share a problematic character, a difficulty or impossibility of simple conclusiveness unless arbitrary imposition is attempted or enforced.

14. For discussions of the *Rhetoric*, see, among others, Robert Bartlett's commentary to his translation; Joe Sachs's introduction to his translations, *Plato Gorgias and Aristotle Rhetoric* (Newburyport, MA: Focus Publishing, 2009); George Kennedy's introduction and notes to his translation, *Aristotle,*

On Rhetoric (Oxford: Oxford University Press, 1991); Martin Heidegger, *Grundbegriffe der aristotelischen Philosophie* (Frankfurt am Main: Vittorio Klostermann, 2002) (a lecture course from 1924); Bryan Garsten, *Saving Persuasion* (Cambridge, MA: Harvard University Press, 2006), chapter 4.

TEN Intellectual Virtue

1. The pleasure of intellectual activity, or philosophy, is presented as seeing or knowing the most noble and divine, not searching for or seeking to know it. Or can searching be an increase in knowing, a partial knowing or observing, even if it falls short of knowledge simply?

2. See *Ethics* I.

3. Book VIII of the *Eudemian Ethics* adds to this discussion. Just as in the whole, everything is moved by soul. The god—the divine—somehow moves all in us: the beginning of reason is superior to it. God is not a ruler as a commander but is the end, that for the sake of which prudence commands. Whichever choosing and acquiring of natural goods most makes for contemplation of the god—bodily goods, wealth, friends, others—is the best and noblest limit. The standard of soul is to be anesthetic of the irrational part of the soul. This is the standard of the gentleman and of the simply good. (We may say that this is to govern passions by virtue in accord with reason—for the noble as well as for the most noble.)

4. Cf. Burger, *Aristotle's Dialogue with Socrates*, 187–88.

5. See Nichols, *Aristotle's Discovery of the Human*, 277. Consider as well the breadth of Aristotle's own works and the matters that must be observed to furnish the evidence on which these works are based. We may suggest that happiness or the most complete end for the composite human being combines the political and the theoretical, ranging in excellence from the philosophical and the political activities (such as Aristotle's architectonic political activities in these works) that are most concerned with beginnings or principles and their order, to the acts of founding or reforming and the philosophical understanding required for this, to the more direct political activities of citizens together with many of the narrower but still philosophical activities that he mentions and in which some of them (and he and his students) are also engaged.

6. On the issue of piety and divinity in the *Ethics*, cf. Nichols *Aristotle's Discovery of the Human*, passim. Aristotle's suggestion (*Ethics* 1179a23–32) that if the gods care for humans it would be reasonable for them to benefit those who, like them, cherish the intellect as well as acting "correctly and nobly" is in its way a downgrading of ordinary virtue and piety.

7. *Ethics* 1152b1–4.

8. See Ethics X, conclusion.

9. *Ethics* 1139a3–1139b4.

10. One might say that the order of understanding is the political philosopher as architect of the end—as understanding ethical virtue, pleasure, activity, nature, intellectual virtue, the justice in the different claims to rule, the city's parts, the modes of persuasion, and the incommensurability strictly of quality and quantity; then a statesman's founding and preserving, which will and needs to grasp most but not all of this, for example, what pleasure and the soul truly are; and then prudence more narrowly as legislative and particular prudence in relation to a particular city.

11. As I have said, seeing this wholeness is also fundamental in understanding animals and their parts.

12. For "whole," see *Metaphysics* V, 26. The similarity between the city's and philosophy's "problematic character" as requiring or expressing both order and disorder is a theme of Michael Davis, *The Politics of Philosophy* (Lanham, MD: Rowman and Littlefield, 1996).

13. As Aristotle also suggests, true arguments and precise distinctions are useful, for when they harmonize with deeds they prompt those who understand them to live in accord with them.

INDEX

MARK BLITZ is the Fletcher Jones Professor of Political Philosophy at Claremont McKenna College. He is the author of numerous books, including *Reason and Politics*.

www.ingramcontent.com/pod-product-compliance
Lightning Source LLC
Chambersburg PA
CBHW060337100426
42812CB00003B/1022